D0214225

THE FRENCH
IN THE UNITED STATES

THE FRENCH
IN THE UNITED STATES

An Ethnographic Study

Jacqueline Lindenfeld

BERGIN & GARVEY
Westport, Connecticut • London

Library of Congress Cataloging-in-Publication Data

Lindenfeld, Jacqueline.
   The French in the United States : an ethnographic study / Jacqueline Lindenfeld.
     p. cm.
   Includes bibliographical references and index.
   ISBN 0–89789–734–X (alk. paper)
   1. French Americans—History. 2. French Americans—Ethnic identity. 3.
  United States—Ethnic relations. I. Title.
  E184.F8L56 2000
  973.04'41—dc21   00–037815

British Library Cataloguing in Publication Data is available.

Copyright © 2000 by Jacqueline Lindenfeld

All rights reserved. No portion of this book may be
reproduced, by any process or technique, without the
express written consent of the publisher.

Library of Congress Catalog Card Number: 00–037815
ISBN: 0–89789–734–X

First published in 2000

Bergin & Garvey, 88 Post Road West, Westport, CT 06881
An imprint of Greenwood Publishing Group, Inc.
www.greenwood.com

Printed in the United States of America

The paper used in this book complies with the
Permanent Paper Standard issued by the National
Information Standards Organization (Z39.48–1984).

10 9 8 7 6 5 4 3 2 1

Contents

Illustrations

Preface

In the early 1990s, some fellow anthropologists encouraged me to undertake a study of the French in the United States, so as to fill a gap in the anthropological literature on ethnicity. I first resisted the idea, arguing that French people who have settled in this country do not really constitute an ethnic group.

However, my own arguments made me reflect on the immigrant experience. What exactly does it mean to be a French-born individual living in the United States on a permanent basis? Is there anything distinctive about the process and outcome of acculturation in French immigrants? Do they maintain their cultural and linguistic heritage? My curiosity had been piqued. I started exploring these issues in informal conversations with natives of France who, like myself, had arrived in the United States as young adults several decades earlier. Our heated discussions led to the design and execution of the research project reported in this book.

As it nears completion, I can look back on an exercise that has been intellectually stimulating and personally rewarding. My thinking about ethnicity has been enriched by it, and I now have a broader view of the French experience in the New World. It is my hope that, despite its limitations, this study will serve to give more visibility to contemporary French immigrants, thus furthering our understanding of the United States as a land of many peoples.

I am greatly indebted to the French-born individuals who allowed me to pry into their lives and willingly answered my questions about the immigrant experience. The data base for this study could not have existed without their gracious cooperation. Their identities will have to remain confidential, but each of them can take pride in having contributed to a fresh source of information on the French population in the United States.

Many thanks are due to friends and colleagues in the United States and France who gave me generous advice and encouragement along the way. Special acknowledgments go to Annick Foucrier for her constant sharing of information about the history of the French in California and her pointed comments on several parts of the manuscript; to Anne Lindenfeld for reading her mother's prose with the sharp eye of an active transmitter of the French heritage; to Richard J. Senghas for his expert advice on some anthropological and linguistic issues covered in this book; and to Romas Simonaitis who, in addition to his constructive critique of each chapter and meticulous preparation of the illustrations, gave me invaluable support whenever the task became overwhelming.

I am grateful to Sonoma State University, particularly the Department of Anthropology and the interdisciplinary Faculty Writing Group, for providing me with an "intellectual home" during the last phase of this project. My presentations of work in progress, either in faculty seminars or in anthropology classes, led to insightful comments by colleagues and students. I am also grateful to the French program and the Department of Behavioral Sciences at Santa Rosa Junior College for their general support of my academic undertakings.

The expert assistance of librarians at Sonoma State University and at Santa Rosa Junior College greatly facilitated my task at various times. Last but not least, Jane Garry deserves recognition for her extremely able editorship and handling of the publication process at Greenwood Press.

Introduction

For Mathilde, the long journey (*"le grand voyage,"* as she called it in French) began a few days after her wedding in Paris, at age 18, to an American who had fought in France during World War I. Upon arrival in the United States, she realized that her life would be changed for ever. "I did not know anything about this country, I did not even know English, it was a case of sink or swim, the beginning of a long journey."

Mathilde was 92 years old when I met her in 1994. At the time, she lived with her daughter in an essentially American environment. However, she "sounded" very French to me, not only in her speech, but also in her way of thinking. How could she have maintained a French identity for 74 years, while manifestly adapting very well to life in the United States?

Acculturation is a complex phenomenon; it consists of multiple layers that can conceal one another. Social integration, an outward manifestation of the adaptation process, must be carefully distinguished from more hidden aspects of existence. This distinction is particularly important in the case of an immigrant population such as the French, whose society of origin draws a clear line between public and private life.

> In some measure, the French have been better placed to resolve the classic dilemma of all immigrants, who must learn somehow to cope with two different and often conflicting ethics. French culture, in France, has characteristically been structured around a blend of public conformity and privatist, individual withdrawal. Because of this innately learned double standard, French immigrants were instinctively better able to be at once thoroughly assimilationist in their business life and intensely French in their private life; though they might not live in French quarters, they would go some distance to buy French bread. (Higonnet 1980: 388)

Apart from carrying a *baguette* (a delightful stereotypical image), what does it mean to remain French in the United States? In order to answer this question, we need factual information derived from empirical research. We need to examine the lives of contemporary French immigrants in some detail. We need to explore the process of acculturation not only in its concrete manifestations, but also at deeper levels of the immigrant experience. We also need to give a voice to the people themselves—in the anthropological tradition of first-hand accounts.

The present study is a step in that direction. It aims at shedding light, on the basis of prolonged ethnographic fieldwork, on a population that remains fairly invisible on the American scene. My specific goal is to present a realistic picture of present-day French immigrants, extrapolating from a representative sample of French-born individuals who reside in this country on a permanent basis.

Given such objectives, it seemed appropriate to adopt a resolutely empirical approach, grounded in methods that are the hallmark of cultural anthropology: direct observation and interviewing. A major source of insight at all stages of this research has been my long history of participant observation, enhanced by insider status, among first-generation French immigrants in this country. However, I have given a central place to ethnographic interviews in my data collection and analysis, in order to avoid unwanted subjectivity.

The systematic collection of interview material took place over a period of three years (1993–1996). Methods ranged from casual conversation to in-depth, focused interviewing facilitated by the use of a standardized set of questions. The target population consisted of French-born men and women who had lived in the United States for a minimum of five years and intended to stay. In order to avoid biasing the sample toward more ethnically involved individuals, I conducted an active search for "isolated" natives of France living among non-

French people, making only minimal use of French organizations to establish contact with potential participants. While this method considerably lengthened the fieldwork period, it provided a diverse sample of French immigrants residing in two western states.

According to the 1990 U.S. Census, California now ranks first in the nation for the number of French-born individuals. My investigation centered on this particular state, with an "incursion" into an adjacent state (Oregon) that offers an interesting contrast since it is far less populated and ethnically diverse. These two western states have the advantage of being located at a good distance from New England and Louisiana, where the French presence has a special history. In addition, the Pacific region is presently of particular interest in the field of ethnicity, due to deep transformations that are rapidly modifying the context for populations of European origin. The recent flow of immigration from Asia—which is second only to immigration from Latin America—and the concurrent development of a "Pacific Rim" ideology have, in the last few years, made Europe appear more and more remote from the West Coast of the United States.

Far from their country of origin, settled in an area in which there are no spatially defined French communities, how do present-day French immigrants residing in the Pacific region experience their lives? What brought them to the United States in the first place? What is their level of integration into American society and their degree of commitment to the French heritage? How do they manage their ethnic identities?

My proposed answers to these questions are based on research informed by various theories of ethnicity. A major source of inspiration was the work of social scientists who regard ethnic identity as a "social construction." Central to this phenomenological conception of ethnicity are people's images of themselves and their dual world; hence the place given in the present study to some perceptual dimensions of ethnicity, in addition to its concrete manifestations.

The first two chapters of this book provide information that serves as background for my analysis. Chapter 1, "Overview of French Migration to North America," contains a historical sketch of the French presence on the North American continent, followed by a census-based picture of the current French population in the United States. Chapter 2, "French Ethnicity on the American Scene," briefly reviews various theories and conceptual frameworks in the field of ethnicity; it also provides a detailed account of my own methods of investigation among French immigrants on the West Coast.

The analysis of the data collected in the field is presented in five central chapters, the sequencing of which was guided in part by temporality. Chapter 3, "Voyage to the West: From France to the United States," presents a general picture of the social background of French migrants to the United States, then retraces the steps of 96 French-born individuals who participated in my systematic interviews on the West Coast. Chapter 4, "Integration into American Society: Socio-Demographic Factors of Acculturation," and Chapter 5, "Life at Home and Beyond: Behavioral and Interactional Factors of Acculturation," deal with overt aspects of the lives of French immigrants in the United States, from food patterns to participation in organizational and community activities. Chapter 6, "Perceptual Dimensions of Ethnicity," explores deeper layers of the immigrant experience, focusing on subjective identity and mental representations in first-generation French immigrants. Chapter 7, "The French Linguistic Heritage," describes language maintenance in the immigrant and subsequent generations, as well as the role of the French language as a marker of ethnicity.

The Conclusion recapitulates the French immigrant experience in the United States, placing it in a broader perspective through brief comparisons with other instances of acculturation in North America and Europe.

1

Overview of French Migration to North America

The paucity of ethnographic material concerning the French in the United States is counterbalanced by a growing number of publications in the field of history. The main sources of information for my brief historical sketch are two comprehensive French-language studies; one of them covers the history of the French in North America (Creagh 1988), and the other one their history in California (Foucrier 1999). Other informative sources are Fohlen (1990), Fouché (1992), Heffer (1989), Heffer and Weil (1994), Higonnet (1980), Hillstrom (1995), Kunz (1966), Morrice (1988), Nettelbeck (1991), Prévos (1997), and Ramirez and Weil (1998).

A HISTORICAL SKETCH OF THE FRENCH PRESENCE ON THE NORTH AMERICAN CONTINENT

The French presence on the North American continent has a long history, which is particularly well documented by Creagh (1988). It begins in the sixteenth century with the expeditions of explorers such as Jacques Cartier, the adventurous forays of fur traders, and the missionary work of Catholic priests. Cartier laid claim to vast territories around the St. Lawrence River in the name of France, but at the time the French government showed no interest in encouraging permanent settlement of its new possessions. However, another Frenchman by the name of Samuel de Champlain further explored parts of present-day Canada in the early seventeenth century, taking the initiative to help establish the first French settlements in Quebec and Acadia to the east.

Throughout the seventeenth century, there were more forays by traders, missionaries, and French explorers into the heartland of North America (Great Lakes region, Mississippi Valley), including Cavelier de la Salle's famous expedition to the Gulf Coast, which resulted in the addition of Louisiana to the French empire in the New World. By then, a number of trading posts in the vast territory named New France had turned into French settlements peopled by "unofficial colonists," who often worked as illegal fur traders and mingled with the Indians. France's interest in extracting wealth from the New World through the fur trade, rather than colonizing its possessions, eventually led to the demise of New France in the late eighteenth century.

The pattern of French colonization had never been as dense as that of the British, due to a lack of strong and consistent support by the French government. As a consequence, most of France's possessions in North America fell into the hands of Great Britain, following several wars that culminated in a British victory and the Treaty of Paris in 1763. By the early nineteenth century, after giving up Louisiana, France had lost its chance to impose itself as a major power in North America.

However, numerous descendants of the first French immigrants still live in parts of Canada, New England, and Louisiana. An important contribution to their numbers was made by highly skilled and prosperous French Protestants who came to the New World in search of religious freedom and economic betterment. Some Huguenots (as they are called) had already taken refuge in the British colonies in the sixteenth century, after years of quarrelling with an overwhelmingly Catholic majority in France, but their efforts to create settlements had not met with success. Conditions were different a century later, as thousands of Huguenots left France—many of them eventually reaching North America—due to the 1685 Revocation of the Edict of Nantes, which had been promulgated in 1598 to protect the rights of Protestants in France. Resolutely turning their backs on a homeland in which they felt unwelcome, these permanent immigrants successfully established their own settlements in the New World. However, they soon gravitated toward English-speaking settlements, using their religious and social background in a markedly skillful manner to blend successfully into the dominant society.

Thanks to their own Protestant ethic of work and perseverance, the Huguenots have left an imprint on American history that is attested, for instance, by the fame of Paul Revere (originally Rivoire in French). Their success story is one of rapid adaptation to the language and culture of colonial American society—in contrast with the course of some early French fur traders, who had adopted the way of life of the Indians and intermarried with them.

In the eighteenth and early nineteenth centuries, the flow of people migrating (on a temporary or permanent basis) from France to the United States was light but steady: military personnel who came to fight under Lafayette in the American Revolution and sometimes decided to stay—as was the case for L'Enfant, the planner of Washington, D.C.; refugees from the French Revolution (such as Dupont de Nemours, the founder of the now famous industrial complex bearing his name) and later from the Napoleonic era; and various individuals who came in search of better lives or simply adventure. At the time, a number of flourishing early French settlements were still in existence, particularly in the Mississippi Valley and the state of New York. French-language newspapers were also still numerous, especially on the East Coast and in Louisiana. But by the late nineteenth century, most permanent immigrants from France residing in those regions of the United States were fast blending into American society.

The West Coast, on the other hand, witnessed the development of thriving French communities between the mid-nineteenth century and the early twentieth century. Three successive waves of immigration from France contributed to this phenomenon, which is richly documented in Foucrier (1999). First of all, the California Gold Rush attracted gold seekers from France, as well as others who provided supplies and services to the miners. There was a high rate of return migration to France, but those who stayed in California were instrumental in creating a critical mass of French immigrants in fast-developing towns such as San Francisco. Second, in the latter part of the nineteenth century, entire groups of people made a collective decision to emigrate from Alsace and Lorraine when these French provinces became part of Germany, as a result of the 1870 Franco-Prussian War. Some of them, especially Alsatian Jews, made their way to places such as Los Angeles. Finally, France participated in a modest way to the large movement of economically induced mass migration from Europe to the United States in the late nineteenth and early twentieth centuries. At the time, French migrants to the New World often used migration chains to leave their villages in poor parts of the country, particularly in the Alps and Pyrénées areas.

In contrast, migration since World War I has most often been an isolated phenomenon propelled by self-motivation, one exception being a wave of (mostly temporary) political refugees during World War II. Chain migration has been rather insignificant in the second half of the twentieth century, due in part to a redrawing of the map of France initiated by the government in the 1960s. An understanding of the significance of this change, which has had a strong impact on movements of people, requires a short detour into French geography.

The historical division of France into provinces (see Map 1.1) is familiar to many people throughout the world: names such as Normandie or Provence are evocative of history, works of art, travel, or cuisine. Less familiar to the outside world is the division of the nation into departments, a classification that came into existence as a result of the 1789 Revolution. At the time it was decided that traditional provinces, whose names and (fluctuating) boundaries evoked despotic power, should be abolished. In a spirit of democratic uniformization, they were replaced by departments of roughly equal size, neutrally named after local topographical features such as rivers or mountains. The latest version of this classification divides the nation into one hundred departments, four of them overseas.

People who live in France are necessarily familiar with this nomenclature, due to its numerous administrative functions and such reminders as postal codes or automobile registration plates. However, the old provinces have never lost their psychological reality. Two centuries after the Revolution, natives of France still tend to respond to inquiries about their regional origins in terms of the traditional provinces, rather than the arbitrarily drawn departments whose names are devoid of historical or cultural significance.

Ironically, the new division of metropolitan France into twenty-two regions, which is based on economic criteria, replicates in part the old division into provinces. Many of the traditional names have been resurrected (or shall we say, maintained), as can be seen by comparing Maps 1.1 and 1.2. The regions, each of which includes two to eight of the existing departments, have been granted increasing administrative functions and more autonomy from the central government in Paris since 1982. The impact of this restructuring has been felt particularly

Map 1.1
France: The Traditional Provinces

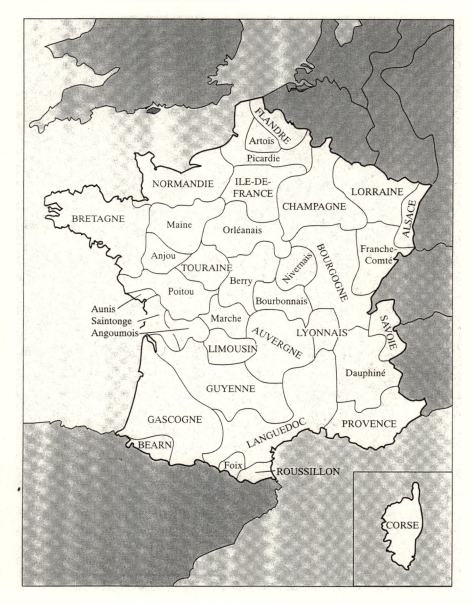

Map 1.2
France: The New Regions

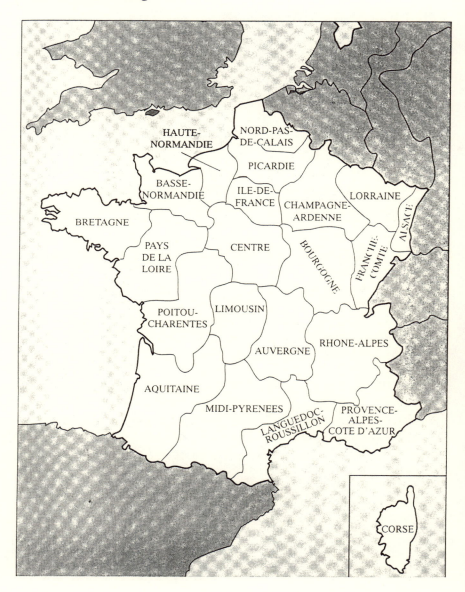

strongly in peripheral areas of France, which are now fully integrated in the national economy.

In several instances, specific changes have also drastically altered local conditions. A good case in point is the former province of Savoie, which is now part of a region named Rhône-Alpes. This area is one of the fastest growing in the nation, having been totally transformed by the construction of dams in the early twentieth century, the exploitation of hydraulic and nuclear energy, and more recently the booming business of ski resorts. Gone are the days of chain migration of Savoyards, either to Paris (where they typically worked as chimney sweeps) or to the New World.

Likewise, the northeastern part of France has undergone profound changes that have put an end to collective migration. Prior to the politically induced exodus from Alsace and Lorraine in the 1870s, there had been some economically motivated chain migration from that area to the United States. But since the end of World War II, the region has enjoyed political stability and increasing economic prosperity, due in part to the prominent role played by Strasbourg (the capital city of Alsace) in the construction and functioning of the European Union. There has been little outmigration from this part of France in the second half of the twentieth century.

Migration trends have also evolved among the Basques, although they remain distinctive within the national context. France, being a prosperous country overall, has never had a strong tradition of economically motivated external migration. While harsh local conditions have, at various points in time, induced some people to leave their places of origin, the pattern has most often been one of internal migration: Inhabitants of poor rural areas tend to go and seek a better life in French cities, Paris in particular. The Basque tradition, on the other hand, encourages external migration, particularly in the case of younger siblings in large farming families, for whom the lack of sufficient usable land is compounded by an inheritance system (primogeniture) favoring elder sons.

Despite the border between France and Spain, strong ties have always existed between French and Spanish Basques. Their long-standing tradition of migration to faraway lands, which was closely tied to Spanish colonialism in the sixteenth century, has created patterns that are not characteristic of the French population at large. In the nineteenth century, migration paths led some Basques first to South America, then to California at the time of the Gold Rush. Their gold mining was not a great success, but it gave them an entry into sheep herding, an occupation to which they brought special skills from their native Pyrénées. It has been said that "no other people became as closely identified with a single economic activity as did the Basques with sheep herding" (Douglass 1980: 176). This occupational niche enabled them to put in place migration chains that soon extended to all the western states. An extensive support system for newcomers from the Basque area gradually developed, and today the Pacific region is still dotted with Basque hotels and restaurants.

The number of French Basques migrating to the United States has reduced drastically in the last few decades, especially since the 1970s due to the steady improvement of local economic conditions. However, some of the long-established patterns, including the use of migration chains from specific Basque villages to the Pacific region, were still in existence in the period immediately following World War II.

THE CURRENT FRENCH POPULATION IN THE UNITED STATES

The long history of the French presence in North America is attested by many place names and a significant number of individuals who claim French ancestry, some of whom live in French-speaking communities. In addition to the widely known case of entire areas in Canada, particularly the province of Quebec, one can think of French settlements still existing in places such as New England and Louisiana. In terms of absolute figures, four of the five counties in the nation with the largest amounts of French ancestry population are located in New England (note, however, that the other one is Los Angeles County); in terms of percentages, all five counties with the highest proportions of French ancestry population in the nation are located in Louisiana (Allen and Turner 1988: 62). In all parts of the United States, including the Pacific region, the French ancestry population ranks among the top ten groups (Lieberson and Waters 1988: 55). The 1,032,843 California residents who reported a French ancestry in the 1990 census represent one-tenth of the national figure (10.3 million).

While census-based rankings shed some light on the French presence in the United States, we should handle the concept of ancestry with great care. Individuals counted as part of the French ancestry population may be several generations removed from their French roots. In addition, they do not all have the same national origins.

> The French-ancestry population includes several groups usually identified more specifically, the two largest of which are those of French Canadian origin and those whose origin lies in a migration directly from France. The patterns of settlement of the two groups are different, and the two were usually members of different social classes and formed separate societies despite a basic similarity in their Roman Catholicism and use of the French language. They seemed to have had different interests and contrasting attitudes towards assimilation into the English-speaking society. (Allen and Turner 1988: 61)

The French immigrants under consideration in my own study came directly from France in the last few decades. I will therefore highlight nativity, rather than ancestry, throughout the remainder of this book. It is also important to bear in mind that native use of the French language cannot be equated with direct French origins; most native speakers of the language residing in the United States actually have Canadian or Caribbean origins. Natives of France differ from them in terms of history, culture, and sometimes even speech patterns. This point recently came to light in Louisiana, when an effort was made to revive the use of the French language by hiring teachers from France for the local schools. The initial lack of success of this program (known as CODOFIL) was due to marked differences, in ways of speaking as well as cultural background, between the French-born teachers and the local population (see, for example, Le Menestrel 1999).

Along the same lines, I will handle the label "French American" with great care, because it is often used loosely. Both in the literature and common parlance, it may designate any type of person with French ancestry, regardless of place of birth, national origins, or the number of generations since departure from France. It may also refer specifically to people of Canadian origin—including Acadians in Louisiana, better known now as Cajuns. These particular groups are most often the only ones represented, to the exclusion of direct immigrants from France, in books and articles entitled "French Americans" in English, or "Franco-Américains" in French (e.g., Parker 1983, Péloquin-Faré 1983, Weil 1989). In order to avoid any ambiguity, I will refrain from referring to direct immigrants from France as "French Americans" whenever possible.

The flow of French immigration has been steady but numerically insignificant in the last few decades. According to the 1997 *Statistical Abstract of the United States*, the yearly average of immigrants from

France amounts to 2,460 for the 1981–1995 period. It is far below the figures for some other European nations, particularly the United Kingdom with its average of 14,900 immigrants per year for the same period of time (U.S. Department of Commerce 1997: 11).

The low rate of recent immigration from France accounts for the relatively small size of the current French population in the United States. The 1990 U.S. Census indicates that it amounts to 119,233 persons, which represents 0.048 percent of the total population, or a ratio of 1 French person to 2,086 U.S. residents. A majority (84,229) of these French immigrants arrived prior to 1980; fewer than one-third (35,004) arrived during the 1980–1990 decade.

The geographical distribution of the current French population reveals a scattered pattern. According to the 1990 census, California now leads in terms of absolute numbers, with 25,507 French-born individuals, or 21.4 percent of the national figure. It is immediately followed by the state of New York (18,411); the next three states are Florida (9,968), New Jersey (6,296), and Texas (5,544).

California had already become one of the major destinations for French immigrants in the nineteenth century, particularly at the time of the Gold Rush; but it is only in recent years that it has outranked the state of New York. It should be noted that, while 17,148 of the French-born residents of California had arrived prior to 1980, the figure for the 1980–1990 decade (8,359) represents about one-third of the total for that state, which is a somewhat higher proportion than the one just cited at the national level. One reason seems to be the lure of the "Golden State" for French people in the last two decades, due in part to the computer industry in Silicon Valley, as documented by Gauchey (1990).

The number of French-born individuals varies greatly from one state to another on the West Coast, as indicated in the 1990 census. Oregon only has 1,104 and the state of Washington 1,593. These low figures may be due in part to the general preference of contemporary French immigrants for heavily populated areas in the United States: Only 12,694 of them live in rural areas in the nation, versus 106,539 in urban areas. In California, the proportions are even more striking: Only 1,487 French-born individuals live in rural areas, versus 24,020 in urban areas.

The numbers can also vary greatly from one county to another. In California, Los Angeles County ranks far above any other, according to the 1990 census, with approximately one-third (8,164) of the total

French-born population in the state (25,507). Next in line are San Diego County with 2,322 individuals, San Francisco County with 2,192, and Orange County with 1,796. However, these absolute figures should be handled with care, since county size is highly variable. In relative terms, Los Angeles County actually has a lower concentration of French-born individuals than San Francisco County (which only includes the city of San Francisco): The French represent 0.09 percent of the total population in the first case and 0.3 percent in the second case.

These figures may seem insignificant, but California appears to be taking an increasingly important place in the history of contemporary French immigration—as attested by the number of new immigrant arrivals from France at selected ports of entry. Data from the Census Bureau indicate that in the year 1996, there were 109 new immigrants from France arriving through Los Angeles and 94 through San Francisco. While New York City still had a higher figure of 234 for that same year, direct immigration to California is a trend that will probably keep increasing in the years to come.

2

French Ethnicity on the American Scene

The complex nature of ethnicity is made readily apparent by problems of nomenclature. Labeling, a deceptively simple matter, can be subject to variation that sometimes reveals deep-seated feelings. French immigrants in the United States are no exception in this regard, as I discovered at a preliminary stage of my investigation. When asked what they call themselves, my interlocutors reacted in different ways. There were assertive responses, such as "I am an American of course," or "I will always be French." There were also hesitant answers: "You might say French American," or "I guess I am both French and American."

The label "French American" currently enjoys a certain degree of popularity among direct immigrants from France, despite its ambiguity (as discussed in Chapter 1). Obviously, this term has the merit of clearly evoking a link between an immigrant's past and present situation. It also offers a parallel with other labels, such as "Japanese American" or "Italian American," which have become familiar to all of us.

However, the appropriateness of the label "French American" was contested by a few of my early interlocutors. "I go back and forth between French and American, mostly I am more French inside and more

American the way I live, it's like two separate identities. So I can't call myself French American, as if the two were really together."

Such comments were valuable pointers to the appropriate framework for my descriptive study of French immigrants. The presence of variation would serve as a major theme, without detracting from the effort to reach generalizations whenever possible. Attention would be given not only to outward manifestations of ethnicity, but also to some of its perceptual dimensions.

In order to reach these goals, I gleaned ideas and methods in an eclectic fashion from the vast literature on ethnicity in the social sciences. Their application to my own research was guided by a desire to validate, through empirical work, whatever generalizations have been or can be made about French immigrants in the United States.

DEFINING ETHNICITY: THEORETICAL AND ANALYTICAL CONCEPTS

In his introduction to *Theories of Ethnicity. A Critical Appraisal*, Thompson (1989) makes some enlightening remarks about the difficult task of defining the concept of ethnicity.

> We have been told that ethnicity is a cultural phenomenon, a political phenomenon, a psychological process, symbolic expression, social organization, and, most recently, a biological phenomenon. Ethnicity is most (though not all) of these things, a fact that accounts in part for the eclectism and obscurantism so prevalent in the field of ethnic relations. (Thompson 1989: 3)

While the charge of "obscurantism" may sound somewhat harsh, there is no question that eclectism has been and remains prevalent in the study of ethnicity for the simple reason that no single theory or analytical framework can possibly cover the whole range of relevant phenomena. Researchers with an empirical bent have therefore not hesitated to use different sources of inspiration, while often adhering primarily to one of the various schools of thought that have guided research in this area for the last few decades.

In North America, three major theoretical paradigms have dominated the study of ethnicity in the twentieth century: assimilationism, cultural pluralism, and so-called variable ethnicity. The first is grounded in an extreme view of the process of adaptation: All individuals in contact with a new society are assumed to eventually reach a stage of total incorporation into it, which in turn completely erases any trace of the native culture (see, for example, Park 1950). It assumes that all immigrant groups automatically undergo a process of homogenization that, sooner or later, brings them into the social mainstream, as they become part of the "melting pot." This image of American society remained mostly unchallenged until the 1960s, despite its failure to account for the persistence of ethnicity in later generations of immigrants.

It took the notion of cultural pluralism to debunk the myth of the melting pot; one of the best known attempts to do so was a book entitled *Beyond the Melting Pot* (Glazer and Moynihan 1963). The pluralist perspective, which highlights ethnic diversity and argues against the inevitable nature of assimilation, is not totally antithetical to that earlier perspective—as shown by Gordon (1964) in his attempted synthesis of these two paradigms into a multidimensional model. However, the heated debate that characterized the 1960s and 1970s led most academics to take sides and exaggerate the differences between assimilationism and cultural pluralism, detracting attention from their common limitations. With hindsight, we are forced to conclude that both perspectives are static in nature and, therefore, inadequate for a satisfactory treatment of ethnicity.

By the late 1970s, it had become obvious to some theorists that monolithic approaches to the study of ethnicity needed to be challenged. In a statement reminiscent of early pronouncements by Barth (1969), the authors of a landmark article note that "rather than an ascribed constant or a temporarily persistent variable, ethnicity and ethnically based ascription are emergent phenomena" (Yancey, Ericksen, and Juliani 1976: 392). They regard the emergence of ethnicity as being intimately linked to structural factors such as the position of a group in a society, as well as the particular circumstances of its members' daily lives, including patterns of social interaction.

The attempt to account for variable ethnicity led researchers in the direction of conceptual models characterized by Gans (1985) as "more situationally sensitive" than the previous ones. Proponents of situational ethnicity highlight the effect of collective or individual circumstances not only on behavioral manifestations of ethnicity, but also on identification at the deeper level. Some of the research conducted in this perspective gives particular attention to the subjective self. Ethnic identity is viewed as a "social construction" of a dynamic nature, grounded as it is in behavior and social interaction, as well as the never-ending process of self-definition.

In the last two decades, researchers have become increasingly aware of the fluid and changing nature of ethnicity within a population or an individual, and much attention has been given to "symbolic ethnicity"— a concept that aptly covers some of the hidden and more subjective aspects of ethnic identity. Social actors are seen as "knowledgeable agents who make their own history, and, as such, play an active role in the construction, destruction and reconstruction of ethnic attachments and identities" (Kivisto 1989: 16). This perspective has been further developed by other authors. In her study of European immigrants living in suburban America, Waters (1990) uses the concept of symbolic ethnicity to refer to the voluntary and episodic nature of ethnic identification in the later generations. Her model highlights the need to examine ethnicity not only in terms of content, but also as a process in which personal choice plays a major role.

The notion of "subjective identity, invoked at will by the individual" (Waters 1990: 7), is appropriate in the case of so-called white ethnics, who can easily blend into mainstream American society. In fact, ethnicity is a somewhat fuzzy concept in the case of people with European origins in the United States. Spindler and Spindler point out that folk definitions distinguish European ethnics and European non-ethnics, the second term being "broadly equivalent to 'mainstream' in the thinking of most people" (1993: 13). However, while "the mainstream is often defined as Anglo-Saxon, North European, and Protestant" (1993: 13), this concept can also be applied to a larger category of "persons of predominantly Caucasian ancestry irrespective of religious identification" (1993: 15).

Such statements echo an earlier comment by Lieberson and Waters concerning "the growth of a population which is quite different from other ethnic groups in the United States. Namely, there are a substantial number of people who recognize that they are white, but lack any clear-cut identification with, and/or knowledge of, a specific European origin" (1988: 264). This point has been further developed by other social scientists in the last decade.

> As social distinctions based on European ancestry have receded into the background, a new ethnic group based on ancestry from anywhere on the European continent has formed. The emergence of this new group, which I call "European Americans," with its own

> myths about its place in American history and its relationship to the American identity, is an important development, with repercussions for racial minorities and new immigrant groups from Asia, Latin America, and the Caribbean. (Alba 1990: xiv)

Where do French immigrants fit in this picture? At a time when France is embarking on a voyage toward European unification, which has begun to obliterate national boundaries, we have compelling reasons to probe the distinctiveness of the French in the United States. Do they simply fall into Alba's proposed category of 'European Americans'? Or do they differ sufficiently from other immigrant populations to be regarded as a separate group? Before attempting to answer such questions on an empirical basis, we need to reflect on the concept of *ethnic group*, which differs in a crucial way from the concept of *ethnic category*.

When referring to the French as an ethnic category in the United States, we are simply saying that they constitute an aggregate of people with common national origins. Nativity, the criterion for membership in this subpopulation, is totally objective and beyond individual control. People who are classified as French in the United States, in a census count or for other official purposes, are simply part of a statistical unit that may have no concrete existence or social identity—in the sense that its members may never be in the same place at the same time and, therefore, may never get to know one another.

While a category may consist of such a random sample of individuals whose only commonality is place of birth, a group "by definition has some degree of coherence and solidarity," and "its members are at least latently aware of common interests" (Petersen 1980: 234). This characterization of the concept of group has the merit of highlighting both its organizational and subjective dimensions. But how do we decide what degree of interaction, coherence and solidarity it takes for an aggregate of people to qualify as a group, rather than a mere category?

In a different perspective, Barth noted long ago that the best way to define an ethnic group is by way of contrast with other groups, focusing on "the ethnic *boundary* that defines the group, not the cultural stuff that it encloses" (Barth 1969: 15). As a precursor of modern theories of ethnicity, he deserves full credit for underlining the crucial role of "self-ascription and ascription by others" (1969: 13) in defining a group.

However, we do not necessarily have to follow Barth in dismissing all traditional ways of measuring ethnicity; trait inventories can still serve a useful purpose in our attempt to differentiate one subpopulation from another. Such a position has been advocated by a number of social scientists in the last two decades. Objective definitions that "require material demonstration of ethnic identity" and subjective definitions that "revolve around ideological positions" are both needed, since "the only satisfactory definition for the participant in ethnic encounters as well as for the analyst is a combination of these two" (Royce 1982: 8). This particular perspective, along with other approaches reviewed here, informed my own investigation of French ethnicity in the United States.

PRESENT-DAY FRENCH IMMIGRANTS ON THE WEST COAST: A DESCRIPTIVE STUDY

The paucity of appropriate ethnographic information on French immigrants in the United States served as a major incentive for the design of the present study. In order to operationalize the concept of French ethnicity, I devised a methodological framework that, while primarily grounded in fieldwork methods familiar to cultural anthropologists, also makes use of some survey techniques favored by sociologists.

Data Collection

Despite the central nature of ethnographic interviewing as a source of findings, it should be kept in mind that direct observation played a crucial role at all stages of my investigation. As an insider, I have been a frequent observer of French people and activities in this country, particularly in the Pacific region, which has been my place of work and residence for more than three decades. Participant observation has been greatly facilitated over the years by personal relations with French immigrants, as well as regular contacts with a number of French organizations, visits to French establishments, and attendance at various kinds of French-sponsored events. This intimate knowledge of the French in the United States, especially on the West Coast, obviously permeates my whole study; but I have used it mostly as a general guide to the understanding of French ethnicity, relying on the interview material as a primary data base for the analysis to be presented in the following chapters.

Ethnographic interviewing was done in three (sometimes overlapping) stages: informal conversations with first-generation French immigrants in the Los Angeles area, beginning in early 1993; systematic interviews with over 100 respondents in southern California, northern California, and southern Oregon over a three-year period, from October 1993 to September 1996; post-interview informal conversations with some of these respondents and other French natives in California and Oregon, during or after the three-year period of systematic interviewing.

The semiformal interviews produced a relatively uniform set of data amenable to both qualitative and quantitative analysis, due to the use of a standardized set of questions. They hold a central place in my descriptive study; however, the value of pre- and post-interview material should not be dismissed. My conversants' informal remarks at all stages of data collection have been a constant source of additional information, as well as a precious safeguard against any unwanted subjectivity on the part of an "insider."

Sampling Procedures

The selection of respondents for the semiformal interviews was based on a combination of random and representative sampling methods. Given my particular interest in "isolated" French immigrants who, on the surface, seem to blend into the American population, I made considerable efforts to locate such individuals through word of mouth or chance co-ethnic encounters, in addition to the occasional assistance of some French organizations. In each of the localities selected as research sites, I enlisted the help of acquaintances, storekeepers or restaurant managers in establishing contact with potential respondents who were strangers to me. Other participants just happened to "cross my path" in various kinds of situations. For instance, a routine servicing visit at a car dealership put me in touch with a French-born cashier who detected my French accent and was eager to chat with a co-ethnic; our conversation led to my request for her participation in this study. A few other respondents were "enlisted" as a result of chance encounters at public events, in leisure activities, or in places such as stores and restaurants. The sample was also gradually expanded through the "snowball approach," as I asked every person interviewed to give me the names of other French people they might know in the community. While these methods prolonged the data collection period, they ensured diversity, as well as a certain amount of randomness regarding the participants' degree of involvement in French organizational life.

The numerous leads to potential participants allowed me to use a combination of random and judgmental sampling methods throughout the data collection period. In order to build a representative sample, I kept in mind the gender dimension, trying to replicate the proportion of two-thirds women to one-third men reported for French-born individuals in the 1990 U.S. Census. Age distribution, on the other hand, was deliberately skewed in favor of middle-age and older respondents, since they would be particularly valuable sources of information regarding the transmission of the French heritage to subsequent generations. As for occupation, it was most often left to chance, but I consciously broadened the range by occasionally approaching individuals engaged in specific activities, such as hotel management, wine making, or the computer industry.

Systematic Interviewing

The interviewing process was preceded by the preparation of an interview guide, a task facilitated by the existence of numerous studies on acculturation. Particularly helpful for the formulation of specific questionnaire items were Bakalian (1993), Stebbins (1994), and Varro (1988).

After drafting a set of questions in French, I enlisted the help of several first-generation French immigrants in order to pre-test the instrument, constantly revising it along the way. One modification consisted of rewriting the interview guide in English, so as to accommodate potential respondents whose native language skills may have deteriorated over the years. It was (correctly) assumed that all participants in this study would have a fairly good command of the English language, having lived in this country for a minimum of five years.

The interview guide, in its final version, consists of 80 items. Questions range in format from structured to open-ended, as illustrated by these two queries: "In what country was your spouse born? USA; Other (specify)"; "Have there been times or circumstances in your life when you have felt more American or more French? Yes/No. If so, please elaborate." The summary that follows will give the reader a preliminary idea of the content of the interview; a complete inventory and exact formulation of the 80 items appear in the Appendix.

A number of questions are demographic in nature: respondent's place and date of birth, marital status, education and occupation; closely related are queries about present citizenship, date of arrival in the United States, and circumstances of emigration—the last one being obviously open-ended. Another set of questions, when applicable, elicits information about the respondent's spouse (national origins, native language) and children (place of birth, gender and age, first language learned).

The major part of the interview is meant to elicit data on behavioral, interactional, and perceptual aspects of ethnicity, with the notion of strategy often functioning as an 'anchor' in the examination of ordinary life situations. The structured or open-ended questions cover three major areas:

- private sphere (family and home): everyday life patterns such as food habits and use of the media; celebration of holidays; language use with various interactants in the home
- public sphere (beyond family and home): participation in French and American organizational and community life, informal social networks, visits to the homeland; language use with various interactants in public
- perceptual and cognitive orientation: mental representations of the United States and France, their societies, cultures and languages, as well as personal preferences regarding the two countries; attitudes toward language, bilingualism, and biculturalism

Other areas covered in the interview deal with issues such as self-labeling and name giving. In addition, respondents were asked to provide detailed reports concerning their own bilingual skills, which I was often able to verify, and those of their spouses and children.

Most interviews were conducted face-to-face in settings that varied according to circumstances: the respondent's home or workplace, a café, restaurant, or public park. I administered the questionnaire myself, taking copious notes on prepared sheets rather than using a tape-recorder (since it had proved somewhat intrusive at the pre-test stage). In southern California, practical considerations forced me to mail questionnaires to a few of the respondents, who filled them out on their own. Incidentally, the rate of nonreturn for self-administered questionnaires (despite their length) was as close to zero as the rate of refusals for face-to-face interviews—an obvious sign of interest on the part of participants in this study.

Many respondents actually expressed their pleasure, in all three geographical locations, in being approached and serving as anonymous representatives of the French population in the United States. They often showed curiosity about the issues we discussed and were extremely generous with their time. The last question in the semiformal interview, "Is there anything else you would like to say about French people in the United States?", occasionally unleashed a flow of additional information, clarifying earlier answers, offering insights into the interpretation of the data, or bringing up new issues.

While French was the main language of communication in pre-and post-interview conversations, the interview itself was usually conducted primarily in English, which gave me a chance to test the respondents' skills in that language. However, a lot of code-switching occurred, particularly when my interlocutors found it easier to answer questions in French or simply felt more comfortable using our common native language. All translations of French language data are mine.

The Final Sample of Semiformal Interviews

I collected a total of 112 semiformal interviews in California and Oregon, 96 of which were later selected for systematic analysis; they constitute the main data base for my descriptive study. Criteria for inclusion in the final sample were as follows:

- The respondent is a first-generation immigrant from France who was a French national at the time of emigration.
- The respondent's early years were spent in an essentially French environment, culturally and linguistically speaking.
- The respondent has lived in the United States for a minimum of five years.
- The respondent plans to stay in the United States.

It was not always possible to screen potential participants for all four criteria before the interview, partly because French standards of politeness make it difficult to ask personal questions in a preliminary conversation. When I occasionally discovered in the face-to-face situation that a respondent failed to meet one or more of the criteria, I proceeded with the interview and put it aside for possible future reference.

A few other interviews also had to be excluded from the final sample due to incompleteness of information, particularly regarding perceptual dimensions of ethnicity. Some respondents found it difficult, not to say impossible, to answer questions about their mental representations of the United States and France, a task that went beyond the sharing of objective information about their lives.

Additional considerations guiding the selection of semiformal interviews for inclusion in the final sample were the respondents' gender, family situation, and geographical location. In each of the three ethnographic sites, the proportion of women to men (two-thirds to one-third) is in keeping with the gender distribution reported earlier for French immigrants at the national level. Family situation refers here to the existence of children and grandchildren; when I had a choice of several interviews for inclusion in the final sample, I gave the preference to those containing information about later generations. As for geographical location, it remained an essential criterion for inclusion in the final sample, particularly in view of my plan to compare two of the three ethnographic sites in terms of organizational and community life, which accounts for the exactly identical number of respondents and gender distribution in two of the subsamples.

The breakdown of respondents is as follows in the final sample of semiformal interviews:

- 18 women and 12 men residing in southern California, most of them in Los Angeles and Orange counties
- 22 women and 14 men residing in northern California, a few in San Francisco, and most in Sonoma and Napa counties in the North Bay area
- 18 women and 12 men residing in Oregon, all of them in Jackson and Josephine counties, an area of southern Oregon known as the Rogue Valley.

These three geographical locations, henceforth respectively designated as L.A. area, Bay area, and S. Oregon, are listed here in the order of their degrees of urbanization and cultural diversity. The first one is a heavily populated metropolitan area with an exceptionally high level of ethnic diversity, in contrast with the Rogue Valley, a semirural area with little ethnic diversity. The Bay area, as defined in the present sample (with most respondents residing in North Bay counties rather than San Francisco), stands between the two others in terms of population density and ethnic diversity.

The 96 respondents included in the final sample cover a wide age range, the youngest being 26 and the oldest 92; the average age is 53.6,

Figure 2.1
Frequency Distribution of Respondents by Age

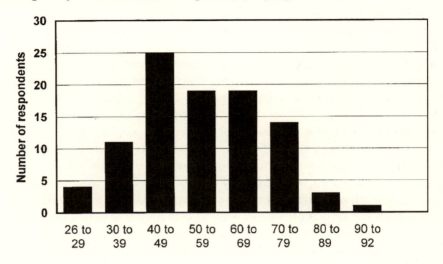

Figure 2.2
Frequency Distribution of Respondents by Date of Arrival in the United States

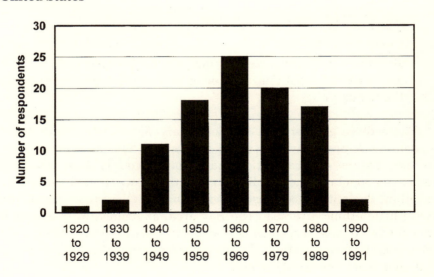

due to the deliberate skewing of my sample toward older individuals. As indicated in Figure 2.1, approximately two-thirds of the respondents (63 out of 96) fall into the 40–49, 50–59, and 60–69 age brackets.

Length of residence in the United States varies from one respondent to another, ranging from 5 to 74 years, with an average of 27.2 years; in almost two-thirds of the cases (57 out of 96), it is 25 years or more. Dates of arrival in this country range over eight decades, from 1920 to 1991, as shown in Figure 2.2. Three respondents came prior to World War II, one in 1920, and two in the 1930s. Eleven arrived in the 1940s, all except one after 1945. Most other respondents came in the 1950s (18 cases), 1960s (25 cases), 1970s (20 cases), and 1980s (17 cases). Two arrived in the early 1990s, respectively 1990 and 1991.

The final sample includes 89 married or formerly married individuals, 77 of whom have children. The number of children per family ranges from one to five, the average being two. Several respondents have grandchildren, and one has great-grandchildren. Many occupational categories are represented, due to the sampling procedures previously described. A detailed picture of the respondents' occupational status will be given in Chapter 4, along with other social characteristics.

Analysis of the Data: A Preview

My interview material constitutes the core of the analysis to be presented in the remainder of this book. Since different methods of analysis were required for the various topics covered, they will be discussed separately in each of the appropriate chapters. It will soon become apparent to the reader that my approach is eclectic and flexible, ranging from qualitative to quantitative methods, as dictated by the nature of the data.

The analysis proceeded along an axis of temporality, which transpires in the chapter organization (as indicated in the Introduction). I tried to reconstruct the *grand voyage* of 96 first-generation French immigrants, beginning with their departure from the homeland and ending with the transmission of the French heritage to their offspring. We follow them through these various stages, gradually gaining a better understanding of the permanent French population in the United States, as we examine the lives of some of its members.

3

Voyage to the West: From France to the United States

In a recent study focusing on transitional stages in the lives of immigrants, acculturation is depicted as a process of second socialization that requires "coming to terms with a new culture after having developed a full personality in the culture of origin" (Hoerder 1996: 212). This is a call for attention to the background of first-generation immigrants, which can have an impact on their adaptation to a new country. Who were they in their homeland? Why did they undertake a voyage that would change their lives for ever?

A consideration of pre-emigration characteristics and motives for departure seems to be an appropriate prelude to a study of acculturation. In this chapter, we first examine these particular aspects of the transition from France to the United States at a general level. Then we turn to individual trajectories of contemporary French immigrants whose voyage resulted in permanent settlement on the West Coast, as documented in my ethnographic data.

GENERAL PRE-EMIGRATION CHARACTERISTICS
AND MOTIVES FOR DEPARTURE

It has become a cliché to say that immigrants come to the United States in search of a "better life." The American Dream is a powerful image: It has motivated millions of people to leave their homelands in order to make better lives for themselves in the "land of opportunity." Some come on their own, others join previous migrants from their local area of origin, hoping to get help in their transition to a new life. The second pattern is prevalent among people from adjoining countries, such as Mexico. As pointed out in a study of Mexican immigrants in southern California, steady social links between specific localities in Mexico and the United States "have developed over generations as part of family strategies for finding alternative sources of income" (Chavez 1998: 12). They result in large concentrations of co-ethnics in specific places that have served as endpoints of migrants' trajectories for many years.

The existence of such migration chains, which has been documented for numerous immigrant populations in the United States, obviously acts as a strong incentive for people to emigrate, especially if they live in economically depressed areas. While France has not been totally exempt from such movements of people in the past, recent trajectories reveal a pattern of predominantly self-motivated migration.

Once they have arrived in the United States, migrants from France tend to maintain an acute sense of self-direction. It can be traced in part to some of their pre-emigration characteristics, for which a thought-provoking historical explanation has been proposed.

> In order to understand the unusual characteristics of French immigration, one must step back and consider briefly the particular evolution of France as a modern society since the 17th century, when migration to America began.
>
> France has always occupied an ambiguous place in the spectrum of modernization. Until very recent times, the French have been a peasant nation: Catholic, rural, hierarchical. But unlike other such countries, France has been at the same time a modern state and in some ways the most modern of all: anticlerical, Cartesian, centralized, bourgeois, and technologically advanced. French history has been uniquely shaped by continual efforts to integrate these contrasting elements—by four centuries of debate between modernizers and traditionalists. (Higonnet 1980: 383)

The concept of modernization certainly has its place in an account of migration from France to the United States. However, we should not overlook the fact that the same features attracting some people to the New World act as repellents for others.

> Some writers have proposed psychological reasons for the French reluctance to desert *la belle France*. In the view of American humorist Andy Rooney, the French have always been masters of finding happiness in their own backyards. Content with their lot, they are rarely tempted to seek a better life elsewhere. A slightly different version of this view holds that the French disapproved of the American way of life, which they saw as worshipping "progress," material goods, and modernization at any cost. Horrified by this society of callous strivers, the French stayed home. The truth of the matter probably touches on all of the above. (Morrice 1988: 69)

We should also not lose sight of many other factors, often linked to life circumstances, in the decision of some French people to settle in the United States. The following characterization of contemporary French immigrants, which has the merit of foregrounding a number of "pull" factors while downplaying the usual "push" factors, served as a blueprint in my ethnographic investigation.

> Most French immigrants in the second half of the twentieth century came to the United States because they married an American citizen or simply wanted to try something different, rather than out of religious, economic, or political necessity. (Hillstrom 1995: 538)

RECENT TRAJECTORIES TO THE WEST COAST

The 96 men and women included in my final sample illustrate many different trajectories from France to the U.S. Pacific region, which made the search for patterns a challenging task. The material collected through systematic interviewing lent itself best to methods of analysis akin to those used in case studies. A number of open-ended questions elicited particularly valuable information regarding the respondents' origins and circumstances of emigration, some of which will be presented in the form of short vignettes.

The individual nature of recent migration from France to the United States is clearly attested in my data: Each of the 96 trajectories represents an isolated case of departure from the homeland. None of the respondents emigrated as part of a group larger than five people or

Table 3.1
Respondents' Regional Origins in France

Region	Respondents (N = 96)
Ile-de-France	29
Rhône-Alpes	9
Provence-Alpes-Côte d'Azur	8
Aquitaine	6
Champagne-Ardenne	6
Bretagne	5
Centre	4
Lorraine	4
Pays de la Loire	4
Alsace	3
Languedoc-Roussillon	3
Midi-Pyrénées	3
Nord-Pas-de-Calais	3
Poitou-Charentes	3
Basse-Normandie	2
Picardie	2
Franche-Comté	2

with people other than relatives. Approximately half of them (47 out of 96) emigrated singly. The remaining 49 came accompanied by a limited number of immediate family members: 44 with French or American spouses, with or without children; 3 with their parents; 1 with her young daughter; 1 with her married daughter and American son-in-law.

The diversity of their local origins also points to a pattern of isolated emigration from France, distributed throughout the country. As indicated in Table 3.1, 17 of the 22 regions of metropolitan France are represented in my sample, which is noteworthy since the respondents' exact places of origin had been left totally up to chance.

Demographic factors obviously play a part in this geographic distribution. The three places of origin with the largest numerical representation in my sample are Ile-de-France, Rhône-Alpes and Provence-Alpes-Côte d'Azur, with 29, 9, and 8 respondents respectively. Ile-de-France (Paris and the surrounding area) is by far the most heavily populated region in metropolitan France, with almost one-fifth of the nation's population. The next two most populated areas are Rhône-Alpes and Provence-Alpes-Côte d'Azur, in that order. By contrast, Corse and Limousin, the least populous regions of France, are not represented in my sample; while these regions have had high rates of out-migration in the twentieth century, the movement of people has been mostly confined to metropolitan France. On the other hand, the three other regions without any representation in my sample (Auvergne, Bourgogne, and Haute-Normandie) are not particularly distinctive in terms of population density within the national context; their absence here must simply be attributed to the random nature of my data collection regarding local origins in France.

A closer look at the respondents' regions of origin reveals that many of them came from especially prosperous parts of the country. We saw that almost half of them (46 out of 96) originated from Ile-de-France, Rhône-Alpes, and Provence-Alpes-Côte d'Azur. These three regions, besides being the most populated in the nation, are at the top of the national economic scale, with Ile-de-France far ahead of any other region. By contrast, the Pyrénées area, which was well known till recently for its economically induced migration patterns, is only moderately represented in my sample: six of the respondents are from Aquitaine (which includes the French Basque area), three from Languedoc-Roussillon, and three from Midi-Pyrénées. Likewise, the sample only includes five respondents from Bretagne, a region that had some economically motivated emigration to the United States until the mid 1960s—and only one of these individuals, who arrived before 1965, corresponds to the picture of poverty stricken rural migrants from that part of France.

The preceding remarks point to the fact that economic factors are not salient in recent patterns of migration from France to the United States. It does not mean, however, that more or less conscious economic considerations are necessarily absent in every individual case. As our examination of some respondents' trajectories will show, reasons for emigrating can be multiple, with a convergence of various "push" and "pull" factors.

We all know that human motivation is an extremely complex phenomenon, which does not easily lend itself to a complete and clear account. Consequently, ethnographers cannot expect to obtain totally unequivocal answers when asking people why they acted the way they did. Even the most cooperative respondents may be unable to sort out the various motives that led them to some major life decision or point to one motive that dominated all others. In the face of such difficulties, I devised two interview questions aimed at eliciting "cross-checking" data from the respondents about their motives for emigration. In the early part of the interview, they were asked to give an open-ended account of their personal circumstances of departure from France (Item #4 in the Appendix). Later on, they had to list any aspects of the homeland that they were happy to leave behind when emigrating (Item #60 in the Appendix). The abundant material elicited in answer to the first question constitutes the main data base for my analysis, while the second set of responses serves as an ancillary source of validation.

Following previous researchers (e.g., Martin and Widgren 1996), I have maintained a strong distinction between economic and non-economic motives for emigration, whether they be push or pull factors, since economics has so often been at the center of migration to the United States. This distinction will readily become obvious in the discussion of my findings.

Throughout the remainder of this chapter, individual trajectories are described in such a way as to preserve anonymity. When information is presented in the form of vignettes, respondents are identified by fictitious names, followed in parentheses by their actual dates of birth and time of arrival in the United States. All summary descriptions are based on the information provided by respondents in my ethnographic interviews, in answer to questions dealing with their motives for emigration or other aspects of their lives. Use of the present tense refers to the mid 1990s, the time when the systematic interviews were conducted.

The "Push" Factors

The individual trajectories of the 96 respondents in my sample are supporting evidence for the general statement made earlier on the basis of their regional origins: In most cases, push factors of an economic nature are not salient in the decision to settle in the United States. Only one-eighth of the respondents unequivocally attribute their emigration to economic conditions in France. Their individual trajectories are presented here in the order of time of arrival in the United States.

Mireille (born 1913, arrival 1950) is partly Basque. She dropped out of school at age 13, in order to help her parents on their small farm in Provence. At age 37, she emigrated to the United States with her partly Basque husband and two young sons, as they despaired of overcoming the economic consequences of World War II. They joined other Basques in Bakersfield, California; she worked in French Basque restaurants before becoming a homemaker, while her husband continued working as a gardener. Now widowed, she has moved to Oregon, where she owns a large house.

Léon (born 1930, arrival 1950) is a Basque from Aquitaine who left school at age 11 to start working as an apprentice to a baker. At age 20, he came to join an uncle in Los Angeles and worked first in a dairy, then in French bakeries. His wife, a Béarnaise who had emigrated from Aquitaine at about the same time, was working as a housekeeper when they met in California. After a while, they decided to start their own business and had successive French bakeries in various locations in the state, all of them successful. They recently sold their latest establishment and are enjoying a well-deserved retirement on their semirural property.

Julien (born 1931, arrival 1950) was part of a large farming family in Midi-Pyrénées and dropped out of school at age 12. At age 19, he came to San Francisco to join relatives who worked in restaurants; they helped him get a job as a cook. He eventually went back to school, earning a degree in horticulture; in his latest position before retirement, he was a landscape supervisor for a school district. He and his American wife, whom he met in California, maintain two homes, one in the city and the other in the country.

Gabrielle (born 1933, arrival 1951) is a Basque from Aquitaine with a ninth-grade education. Her parents were very modest farmers, and several of her brothers emigrated to the United States for economic reasons. One of them, who worked as a shepherd in Montana, helped her locate a job as a housekeeper when she was 18. She later moved to California and married a British-born American. Her jobs have included waitressing and office work; her husband works in the insurance industry.

Rémi (born 1918, arrival 1962) was born and raised in Paris. He dropped out of school at age 11 to start working as a mechanic. After World War II, the housing crisis made it very difficult for him to provide adequate housing for his French wife and three children; so he decided at age 39 to emigrate to Canada, where he found a job as a mechanic. His family joined him, and five years later they moved to California, where he continued working as a mechanic. He and his wife are now retired and live in their own modest home.

Odette (born 1921, arrival 1962), the wife of Rémi above, was born and raised in an impoverished rural part of Bretagne; she has an eighth-grade education. After joining her husband in North America, she worked for many years as a housekeeper, in order to help provide for the family.

Patrice (born 1940, arrival 1968), who comes from the Rhône-Alpes region, has a ninth-grade education and a vocational degree in cooking. He started working as a cook at age 15, then decided at age 22 to migrate to the United States for better economic opportunities. As an experienced chef, he has always been able to find work and now owns and runs an upper-scale French restaurant in Oregon with his American wife.

Liliane (born 1949, arrival 1968) had an eighth-grade education when she met her American spouse on a U.S. military base in her native Lorraine. After their marriage, her husband worked in her father's plumbing business for a few years. But the low pay and harsh working conditions made them decide to move to California (his native state), where he has been able to use his training as an engineer. While raising their two children, she completed her high school education and went on to college, earning a bachelor's degree that led first to office jobs, then to her current teaching position.

Sébastien (born 1947, arrival 1969) is a Basque from a large farming family in Languedoc-Roussillon. He has a ninth-grade education and a vocational degree in cooking. At age 22, he came to the San Francisco Bay area, where close relatives who owned Basque restaurants gave him a job. His wife, whom he met in California, is of French parentage. They have had their own Basque restaurant, a highly successful establishment, for two decades.

Corinne (born 1957, arrival 1982) is from Rhône-Alpes. After completing a college degree in political science in France, she was not able to find employment. At age 25, she decided to go to Los Angeles and work toward a bachelor's degree in cinematography, which readily opened doors for her. She now works there as an assistant film editor.

Gérard (born 1938, arrival 1955, back in France 1966–1986, second arrival 1986) grew up in the Paris area, then migrated to the United States with his parents at age 17. After obtaining a degree in commercial designing, he went back to France and settled into family life. However, the deteriorating economic conditions and rising unemployment rate made him decide to leave France again in 1986. Some relatives in California helped him start a new career as a distributor of specialty foods.

Christian (born 1959, arrival 1991) is from Paris. After obtaining a college degree in journalism in France, he experienced long periods of unemployment as a freelance writer. He came to the United States at age 32 in search of better opportunities and has been working as a journalist in southern California ever since.

The last three individuals (Corinne, Gérard and Christian) fall into a special subcategory: Despite their higher education degrees, they were directly affected by the serious unemployment crisis that France has been undergoing since the mid 1970s. If my sample had not been deliberately skewed in favor of older people (for reasons indicated in Chapter 2), it would undoubtedly have included more respondents who left France in such conditions. The 1980s and 1990s have witnessed an influx of (mostly young) French people with qualifications who come to large American cities in search of jobs; however, it is impossible to know how many of them will eventually decide to settle permanently in this country.

Let us return to the first nine individuals (Mireille, Léon, Julien, Gabrielle, Rémi, Odette, Patrice, Liliane, Sébastien) whose trajectories were briefly described. It is noteworthy that all of them emigrated with a limited amount of formal education—a definite handicap in a degree-obsessed nation such as France. A related feature is that six of them were members of poor or modest families in rural parts of Bretagne (Odette) or the southernmost regions of France (Mireille, Léon, Julien, Gabrielle, Sébastien), in contrast with many other respondents in my sample who have middle-class origins and came from richer urbanized areas. Finally, we should note that Léon, Julien, Gabrielle, and Sébastien, all of whom are Basques, as well as Mireille who is partly Basque, had help from close relatives and/or other co-ethnics in the United States when they arrived. No other respondents in my sample reported using such networks, which attests to the exceptional nature of the persistence of Basque migration chains in the 1960s.

We will return to economics when discussing pull factors in the next section; let us for now dwell a little longer on push factors. Besides those of an economic nature, the most common have been, historically speaking, politics, religion, and war. The role of such factors is minimal in the case of contemporary French migrants to the United States, as noted by Hillstrom (1995) and attested by my sample.

Political motives were never mentioned in the course of my systematic interviews as a primary motive for emigration. While a few respondents expressed a certain degree of dissatisfaction with French politics, it had to do with the general situation in France, rather than any specific political figure or event. As for religious motives, they were salient in only one case in my data, and the voluntary nature of the respondent's departure from France must be underlined.

Yann (born 1953, arrival 1977) converted to the Mormon religion while still living in his native Bretagne. At a certain point, the absence of a critical mass of adherents to his religion in France made him decide, on his own, to go and live in the United States, where he made a career change. He and his wife, an American of French-Canadian ancestry from New England, continue to practice the Mormon religion in Oregon.

We saw earlier that war was an indirect cause of departure from France in three of the twelve cases of economically induced migration. Mireille and her now deceased husband left Provence because of the general harsh economic conditions resulting from World War II; as for Rémi and Odette, they had been directly affected by the postwar housing crisis in Paris. My data also contain two instances of departure from France that are directly attributable to the war; however, personal considerations of a psychological nature seem to have overridden economic motivation in each of these two cases.

Maurice (born 1926, arrival 1953, back in France 1955–1962, second arrival 1962) had a promising future in Paris as an upper-middle class law student with a position in a law firm. At age 27, he came to the United States on a trial basis, wanting to get away from sad personal memories of the war. After a few years back in France, he returned to help an American friend start a coffee shop on the West Coast, a risky venture financially speaking. He never resumed his legal career in France. By now, he and his American wife have several successful establishments in California.

Isabelle (born 1936, arrival 1958) had a difficult childhood and adolescence in Provence. Her father, an officer in the French army, died early in the war, leaving behind a Japanese wife who was made to feel an alien in wartime France. At age 22, as a third-year college student majoring in English, Isabelle decided to visit some relatives of her mother's in California, in order to take some distance from her sad family situation. After a year of temporary teaching, she returned to France for a few months, then enrolled in a master's program at a midwestern university, where she met her American husband. Her teaching career on the West Coast corresponds more or less to the career she would have had in France.

My data contain two other instances of departure from France in which push factors of a clearly personal nature played a central part. One female respondent emigrated at age 19 in order to avoid an arranged marriage; another emigrated with her young daughter in order to escape harassment by her estranged husband. In each case, the presence of French relatives in California acted as a pull factor in the choice of a destination.

No other respondents in my sample clearly indicated that major push factors played a part in their decision to settle in the United States. This overall picture appears to be corroborated by responses to my question about any aspects of France they were happy to leave behind (Item #60 in the Appendix).

It is rather significant that 27 of the 96 individuals interviewed had nothing to report along those lines. Many of them had left France under the influence of pull factors (to be examined in the next section), rather than fleeing from conditions in France that they did not like. In fact, several French women who had met their American husbands overseas expressed some regret, despite their fulfilled lives in the United States, about having left France as young adults.

As for the comments made by the remaining 69 respondents about negative aspects of life in France, they range in topic from the social climate to such mundane features as shopping habits. In the following inventory of their multiple responses, I have listed topics and subtopics in order of frequency of occurrence, with the numbers in parentheses indicating how many times each particular category of comments is represented in the data:

- general lack of freedom (19 tokens): too many rules, constriction and narrow-mindedness, discouragement of initiative
- the French character (14): arrogance, tendency to be critical, pessimism, morosity, pettiness
- organizational structure (12): too much bureaucracy, lack of efficiency and discipline in the workplace
- the political situation (11): too much governmental interference, too many taxes, too many strikes
- the economic situation (9): lack of jobs and opportunities, unemployment especially for young people
- overemphasis on tradition (9): excessive focus on the family, importance given to table manners and other constraining rules

- social stratification (7): rigid class system, too many social barriers, too much inequality
- racism and xenophobia (7): anti-Semitism, negative attitudes toward foreigners
- material aspects of life (7): lack of space, lack of comfort, constraining shopping and eating habits
- wartime (6): resulting economic or personal difficulties, scarcity of adequate housing

This brief inventory seems to indicate that French immigrants currently living in the Pacific region, while they may have been critical of France in some ways, did not profoundly dislike their homeland when they departed. It confirms that most of them, rather than fleeing an unbearable situation (the push effect), were simply drawn to the United States by a number of positive factors (the pull effect). What exactly could have motivated these predominantly young French men and women to undertake their voyage to the West, leaving behind a generally prosperous country and familiar social networks?

The "Pull" Factors

My empirical data strongly support Hillstrom's observation regarding the saliency of marriage as a motive for migration from France to the United States in recent times. Approximately one-fourth (23 out of 96) of the respondents in my sample came to this country as a result of marriage to an American. These 19 women and 4 men met their future spouses in France (20 cases), North Africa (2 cases), or Switzerland (1 case). A total of eight women are war brides: one from the World War I period, two from the World War II period, and five from the period immediately following WWII when numerous U.S. military bases were located in France and nearby.

In addition, the marriage factor (which will be examined more closely in Chapter 4) is often present in the case of other respondents who arrived singly in the United States, either to pursue some studies or as a result of a job offer or company transfer, and eventually settled here. However, it is often difficult to disentangle the various factors involved in such instances of inadvertent emigration: There can be an overlap of personal considerations and economic motivation, whose relative weight is not always clear even to the people themselves. A perfect example is the case of a single young adult who moves to the United States as a student, with the firm intention to go back to France after a while, but lets life take its course. My sample includes nine women and five men who, in their late teens or early twenties, went to the United States for a temporary program of studies (in some cases under the Fulbright program) and are now settled in this country. All 14 are pursuing careers directly related to their American degrees, and 12 have married Americans whom they met over here.

Pull factors of a clearly personal nature are present in two other cases involving particular family situations: one widowed woman came to join her daughter who had married an American in France and emigrated a few years earlier; one divorced woman came along with her daughter who had married an American stationed at a military base in North Africa.

The remaining cases in my data represent a complex mixture of motives for emigration. Several respondents perfectly illustrate the "modernizer" type discussed earlier: They arrived with education and skills in this country, as well as a strong desire for personal achievement in a social context that favors initiative, free enterprise, and flexibility. While the lure of better career opportunities and a higher standard of living may have played a role in their decision to settle here, these entrepreneurial individuals seem to have had a particularly strong attraction to the open environment characteristic of the United States.

Arnaud (born 1949, arrival 1969), who grew up in Paris, already had thoughts of leaving France as a young teenager. His mother, who was about to migrate to the United States as a young adult when marriage altered her plans, raised him with the idea that his future was there. After completing high school in France, he decided to "start a new life" in Los Angeles, holding a job while working toward degrees in finance, real estate, and international business management. His impressive background has made it easy for him to obtain responsible positions in banking or real estate in California and Oregon.

Serge (born 1952, arrival 1974) grew up in Provence and completed high school in France, as well as a higher education vocational degree in hotel management in Switzerland. Over the years, his parents had strongly influenced him to leave France and its system of "heavy governmental interference." At age 22, he came to the United States by himself on a one-way ticket, determined to make a life for himself in the United States. He concurrently worked in hotel management and completed his B.A. and M.A. degrees on the East Coast. He then worked in several places on the West Coast and met his American wife. He is now at the head of an expanding hotel chain in several western states.

Bertrand (born 1954, arrival 1979) grew up in the Rhône-Alpes region. After obtaining a higher education degree in business management, he started working for Royal Viking Lines. Since their cruise ships are based in San Francisco, he got a taste of the American way of life and, like many of the other employees, found himself yearning to live in this country. He married an American tourist from Arizona and lived in that state for a while. Later on, he moved to the West Coast, where he has held managerial positions in high class hotels, restaurants, and country clubs.

Loic (born 1955, arrival 1984) is from Bretagne. He came to California at age 29 with his French wife and child, when a job offer gave them the chance to realize their dream. He and his wife had always wanted to come and live in the United States, "where individual initiative is encouraged and parents have more of a voice in their children's school activities and learning." They are happily settled in a country that has provided them not only with good economic opportunities (they now manage a hotel and a spa), but also with the kind of family lifestyle they had envisioned for themselves.

Other respondents, whose careers have had more moderate proportions, seem to have been guided primarily by a desire for change and excitement in their personal lives, rather than being particularly attracted by modernization or the prospect of "endless" economic opportunities. Their voyage to the West most often began as a temporary venture, which turned into a permanent one due to various life circumstances and their sense of self-direction.

Sophie (born 1936, arrival 1961), who had a responsible position in marketing in Paris, was sent to New York at age 25 by her employers who wanted her to learn English. They had placed her in a temporary *au pair* position in New York, but she soon decided to strike out on her own, locating a regular job which allowed her to stay longer than originally planned. She eventually settled in California after marrying an American.

Bernadette (born 1931, arrival 1963), a woman with vocational degrees and a good position as head of a child care center, decided at age 32 to leave France "for a change." She located a job in a clinic in California, came with a five-year visa, and ended up staying for a lifetime because she married an American.

Véronique (born 1932, arrival 1968) grew up in the Centre region of

France. She completed high school and two years of college, then married a Frenchman and had two children. After her divorce, she trained as a dental assistant and worked for a dentist in Paris who encouraged her to go to the United States "for a change." Leaving her young children in her mother's care, she went to New York by herself and soon found a job in a dental office. A few years later she came to California, where she has been moving from one dental office to another with the confidence of someone who trusts her luck.

Hervé (born 1948, arrival 1971), whose roots are in Bretagne, was "imported" by an American circus for his horseback riding performance at age 23. While growing up in a consistently French home and school environment, he had lived in Denmark, Indochina, and Africa with his parents for a few years. As a result, he was prepared to accept a job offer that would open up his horizons even further. He has adapted very well to life in California, using his multiple skills to build a diversified career for himself.

Jérôme (born 1954, arrival 1979) grew up in the Franche-Comté region. After completing high school and a vocational degree in horticulture, he came to San Francisco in order to perfect his English, working as an *au pair* and chauffeur. He then went to South America on a six-month backpacking trip, returned to San Francisco, married an American, worked for a newspaper for two years, took off for a prolonged trip around the world, and finally settled into a permanent Post Office job in California.

Pascal (born 1960, arrival 1983) grew up in the suburbs of Paris. After obtaining a vocational degree in pastry making, he managed to get a job with Club Méditerranée "in order to see the world." At age 23, he went to Florida on a tourist visa and found a job as a pastry maker, which allowed him to stay. He then moved to Arizona, married an American, and lived there for a while. They subsequently spent four years in Polynesia, where he worked as a U.S. licensed pilot for a private airline while his wife worked as a speech therapist. Upon returning to the United States, they first lived in Utah, then moved to Oregon where they are raising two children. He presently is a freelance pastry maker and "house husband."

Sylvie (born 1968, arrival 1987) came to the United States at age 19 because of her passion for horses. Through her horseback riding activities in France, she met some people who offered her a summer job on a horse ranch in California, and the temporary job lasted three years. She went back to France for a year, returned to the same ranch in

California, met her American husband, and finally settled here. She now has a permanent job on a horse ranch, the dream of her life.

These examples illustrate the significance of clearly personal reasons, linked to life circumstances, in the decision of some French-born individuals to settle in the United States. Their sense of adventure, desire for change, and curiosity about North America are well summarized in the words of Irène, an 89-year-old respondent who emigrated to Canada in 1932 at age 24 with her French husband and two young children, then came to the United States a few years later. "At first I was reluctant to leave France, you know, all my relatives and friends. But my husband really wanted to go, so I became curious about Canada and the United States. And then, you know, we were young and adventurous. So off we went, just for a change!" A voyage which would turn into a lifetime in North America.

4

Integration into American Society: Socio-Demographic Factors of Acculturation

Once their voyage to the West turns into permanent settlement in the United States, how do French immigrants fare in American society? In this chapter, we examine some socio-demographic features that are commonly used as indicators of acculturation: residence and marriage patterns, socio-economic characteristics, and citizenship status. Each of these factors will be considered in turn, with frequent reference to their interplay, as well as gender differences. The next chapter will deal with closely related factors of acculturation, namely behavioral and interactional aspects of life at home and beyond.

Conspicuously absent from this chapter is a detailed examination of such formal institutions and mechanisms as church, school, and politics, which often receive much attention in the study of ethnicity. Their role is minimal in the case of direct immigrants from France presently living in the United States, for reasons which will be made clear in Chapter 5.

RESIDENCE AND MARRIAGE PATTERNS

Recent trajectories from France to the United States, as described in Chapter 3, perpetuate the pattern of geographical dispersal that has

Figure 4.1
Marital Status by Gender

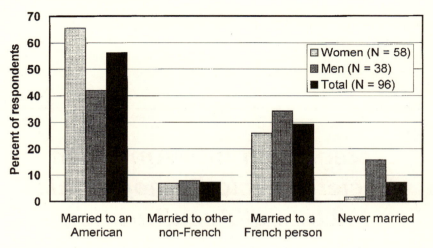

characterized French immigration at various times in American history. Preliminary destinations are most often determined by individual factors, the result being likely isolation from compatriots. This situation is compounded by the absence, at the present time, of spatially defined communities populated by direct immigrants from France.

A direct consequence of this lack of territorial identity, combined with the small size of the French population in the United States, is that migrants from France come in frequent contact with Americans. For those who emigrated singly, it often leads to intermarriage. Recent census figures indicate that, in comparison with some other immigrant populations from Europe whose native language is not English, the French have a particularly high incidence of intermarriage.

Their notable exogamy rate is well attested in my ethnographic data, as shown in Figure 4.1. The final sample of 96 respondents includes 61 individuals who have (or had, if currently widowed, divorced, or separated, and not remarried) non-French spouses; 54 of these non-French spouses are American, and 7 are other non-French nationals. The remaining respondents divide into 7 never-marrieds, and 28 who have (or had, if currently widowed, divorced, or separated, and not remarried) French spouses; only 4 of these 28 inmarried individuals met their spouses in the United States after immigration.

Figure 4.1 also indicates that exogamy is even more frequent among the 58 female respondents in my sample than it is among the 38 male respondents. While 65.5 percent of the women are married to Americans and 6.9 percent to other non-French nationals, which amounts to a total exogamy rate of 72.4 percent, the corresponding figures for the men are 42.1 percent, 7.9 percent, and 50 percent. Conversely, only 25.9 percent of the women are married to French persons, versus 34.2 percent of the men. The remaining 1.7 percent women and 15.8 percent men have never been married.

Approximately two-thirds of the 61 respondents who are members of mixed couples met their non-French spouses in the United States. In those cases, adaptation to American life was a gradual process that had already begun before marriage. On the other hand, there was a somewhat abrupt transition for the 19 women and 4 men who had met their American spouses in France, Switzerland, or North Africa. A few of them had some exposure to American life before emigration due, for instance, to the presence of a U.S. military base in their area. Others, however, had no such experience and hardly knew what to expect in America. Acculturation often had to be an accelerated process, particularly for those who started families almost immediately after arrival and were not always able to maintain close contact with the homeland. Such was the case for Mathilde, the previously mentioned female respondent who came at age 18 as a non-English-speaking WWI bride, at a time when intercontinental travel and communication facilities were not what they are today.

Intermarriage has been characterized as "both an indicator of the degree of assimilation of ethnic and racial groups and an agent itself of further assimilation for the couples who intermarry and for the next generation" (Lieberson and Waters 1988: 162). The high outmarriage rate of French immigrants can certainly be considered as both a predictor and an agent of acculturation, not only for the first generation, but also—and even more so—for later generations. My ethnographic data contain only two reported instances of marriage with French nationals in the immigrant generation's offspring, and one of marriage with a French Canadian.

Such patterns result in part from demographic factors (namely group size and geographical distribution) that "increase the propensity toward outmarriage by weakening ethnic attachments *and* by increasing contact with potential mates from other groups" (Lieberson and Waters 1988: 211). But the high intermarriage rate of the French population must also be attributed to societal forces that set it apart from some other immigrant populations. The significance of individual decision making in the lives of first-generation French immigrants, which is clearly documented in my ethnographic data, precludes the imposition of an inmarriage model on their children.

Intermarriage can play a major role in the acculturation process, as "a potentially important factor working against the long-run maintenance of the group as a separate entity" (Lieberson and Waters 1988: 165). Its impact is particularly strong in the case of immigrants whose socio-economic characteristics favor contact with the outgroup, which is the case for the French in the United States.

SOCIO-ECONOMIC CHARACTERISTICS

A common characterization of French immigrants in the literature is that they "have tended to be more successful and influential than other groups in America" (Hillstrom 1995: 537), as demonstrated by their numerous contributions to various domains of society over three centuries. The success of this "atypical" immigrant population has been attributed to the "consistently middle class and skilled" background of its members (Higonnet 1980: 383).

There is no question that the Huguenots, and many other French immigrants after them, were helped by their social origins in the process of integration into American society. However, we must beware of the "mirage" created by the high visibility of some illustrious individuals. We cannot overlook the fact that, over the centuries, French migrants to the United States have constituted a diverse population (Creagh 1988: 473).

My own ethnographic data reveal a variety of social backgrounds, as indicated earlier. Overall, they correspond to general emigration records for modern-day France, which show an over-representation of the professions and business and an under-representation of farming. However, we discovered that several participants in my study, who emigrated for primarily economic reasons, had rural or working-class origins associated with limited schooling. The sample also includes women who had relatively low levels of formal education or occupational skills when they met their American husbands overseas; this is particularly true of the war or post-war brides of U.S. servicemen, several of whom were teenagers at the time of marriage. While most respondents in my sample have achieved various degrees of socio-economic success in the United States, regardless of social origins in-

France, it often results from great efforts on their part to improve their social standing after immigration—a fact that needs to be recognized.

An important consideration in this regard is the possibility for individuals to enter the American work force with limited formal education, then steadily improve their occupational status through further education or the development of specific occupational skills. The success of French migrants who settle permanently in the United States is based in part on their eagerness to keep learning, as attested by the fact that many of them enroll in programs of studies in American institutions of learning. This is the case not only for those who came specifically to pursue a program of studies, but also for others who decided to attend college at some point in their adult lives—an opportunity they may not have had in France, where higher education is oriented mostly to young people.

The pursuit of further education, which plays a definite role in occupational advancement and integration into American society, is highlighted here through a comparison of the participants' levels of education at two different stages: before immigration and at the time when I interviewed them. We will also examine gender differences in educational attainment before and after immigration.

Figure 4.2 shows a broad range of pre- and post-immigration educational attainment in the 96 respondents, from a sixth-grade level to five or more years of higher education. Pre-immigration levels are sixth- to ninth-grade for 20.8 percent of the sample, tenth- or eleventh-grade for 11.4 percent, and twelfth-grade (completion of high school or equivalent) for 32.3 percent, which means that a total of 64.5 percent of the participants had no college education when they emigrated. Among the pre-immigration college educated respondents, who constitute the remaining 35.5 percent of the sample, 14.6 percent had one to three years of higher education before arriving in the United States, 16.7 percent had four years, and 4.2 percent had five or more years.

The post-immigration figures reveal an almost exact reversal of these proportions: 35.4 percent of the participants have a sixth- to twelfth-grade education, while 64.6 percent are college educated. This dramatic shift is due primarily to a sharp decrease—from 32.3 percent to 7.3 percent—in the proportion of respondents with a twelfth-grade education, many of them having attended college in the United States after immigration. As a consequence, the percentage of respondents with four years of higher education has increased from 16.7 percent before immigration to 28.1 percent after immigration, and the proportion of

Figure 4.2
Educational Attainment by Gender

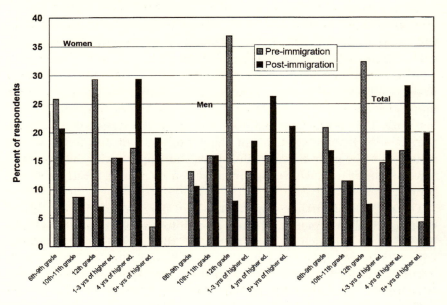

those with five or more years of higher education has shifted dramatically from 4.2 percent before immigration to 19.8 percent after immigration. This last category is composed of 3 individuals who already had advanced degrees upon arrival in the United States and 16 who obtained master's or doctoral degrees (11 and 5 cases respectively) after immigration.

This comparison of pre- and post-immigration levels makes it clear that obtaining further education has been a major preoccupation for participants in my study. While this is especially true of those who already had a twelfth-grade education before coming over, it should be pointed out that four individuals who emigrated with an eighth- or ninth-grade education have gone back to school and obtained either a General Educational Development certificate (1 case) or a college degree (3 cases). On the other hand, the 11 respondents who emigrated with a tenth- or eleventh-grade educational level have not sought further education in the United States; most of them had received vocational training during their last two years of school in France, acquiring marketable skills in areas such as cooking, child care, or mechanics.

The gender distribution shown in Figure 4.2 reveals few significant differences between the female and male respondents, both before and after immigration, in terms of the global categories of college educated and non-college educated individuals: 36.2 percent of the women versus 34.2 percent of the men had some college education prior to immigration; 63.8 percent of the women versus 65.8 percent of the men have post-immigration college education. Therefore, the non-college educated include 63.8 percent of the women versus 65.8 percent of the men prior to immigration, and 36.2 percent of the women versus 34.2 percent of the men after immigration.

Among the college educated, there is no major gender-based difference in any of the subcategories (1–3 yrs of higher education, 4 yrs, 5+ yrs) before and after immigration. Among the non-college educated, on the other hand, many more women than men at both stages have a sixth- to ninth-grade education, whereas fewer women than men have a tenth- to eleventh-grade or twelfth-grade education. A number of the female participants in my study are old enough (up to 92 years of age) to have been raised in France at a time when education was not yet compulsory past age 13 and when some families were inclined to think that a girl's education was less important than a boy's. Several of the 15 women with a pre-immigration sixth- to ninth-grade educational level married Americans at a young age and became homemakers; only 3 of those went back to school while raising children, earning either a General Educational Development certificate or an associate or bachelor's degree.

High educational qualifications and specific skills often lead to correspondingly good occupational opportunities in the United States, a pattern that clearly emerges from my data. At the time of the interviews, all respondents except for nine homemakers were (or had been, if retired) engaged in some occupation. For eight of the nine homemakers, having no occupation was a personal choice; only one was involuntarily out of the labor force while looking for an appropriate job, after giving up a good position in France in order to follow her American husband.

In my categorization of the respondents' occupations, which is shown in Figure 4.3, the working respondents' current occupations and retired respondents' most recent occupations have been aggregated, since the goal is to illustrate the range of occupational statuses among first-generation French immigrants in the last few decades.

All major occupational categories are represented to varying degrees in my sample. The three categories that stand at the upper end of the

Figure 4.3
Occupation by Gender (percent)

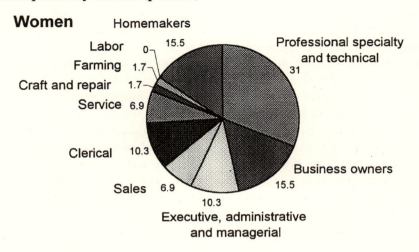

Women

Homemakers
15.5

Labor 0
Farming 1.7
Craft and repair 1.7
Service 6.9

Clerical 10.3

Sales 6.9

Professional specialty
and technical
31

Business owners
15.5

10.3

Executive, administrative
and managerial

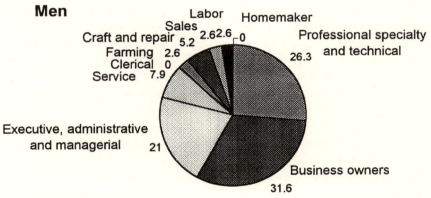

Men

Labor   Homemaker
Sales 2.6 2.6 0
Craft and repair 5.2
Farming 2.6
Clerical 0
Service 7.9

Professional specialty
and technical
26.3

Executive, administrative
and managerial   21

Business owners
31.6

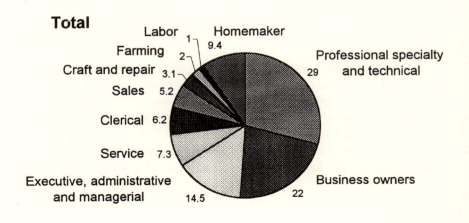

Total

Labor   Homemaker
1   9.4
Farming 2
Craft and repair 3.1
Sales 5.2

Clerical 6.2

Service 7.3

Executive, administrative
and managerial   14.5

Professional specialty
and technical
29

Business owners
22

socio-economic scale in the United States are particularly well represented: 29 percent of the respondents fall into a category that can be labeled professional specialty/technical, 22 percent are business owners, and 14.5 percent have executive/administrative/managerial occupations—a combined total of 65.5 percent of the sample. The remaining respondents who have occupations fall into the following categories: 7.3 percent in services, 6.2 percent in clerical occupations, 5.2 percent in sales, 3.1 percent in craft and repair, 2 percent in farming, and 1 percent in labor. Homemakers represent 9.4 percent of the total sample.

The broad occupational array just described may derive in part from my methods of data collection. As mentioned in Chapter 2, I used a combination of random and judgmental sampling in order to locate potential respondents for the systematic interviews, occasionally making deliberate efforts to find representatives of specific occupations. This was the case in particular for certain occupational niches, such as hotel management and the food industry, which have been important in the history of French immigrants to the United States. As for the high number of respondents in the professional specialty/technical and the executive/administrative/managerial categories, it may be partly attributable to their high visibility in the community, which made them easier to locate than some other French individuals. However, I tried to counteract this potential bias by giving a large place to "chance encounters" in my panoply of field methods—as described in Chapter 2. In this regard, it is interesting to note that the picture emerging from my data corresponds closely to the following portrayal of post-WWII French immigrants, which appeared in print after completion of my semiformal interviews.

> Many French who immigrated to America after 1950 were active in teaching and abstract research (in secondary schools and universities), business and commerce (restaurant owners, chefs, designers), and industrial or applied research (computer specialists, software designers). (Prévos 1997: 290)

We can refine this portrayal by highlighting the gender distribution in the occupational composition, as it appears in my sample. Figure 4.3 indicates that 56.8 percent of the women and 78.9 percent of the men fall into the three occupational categories at the upper end of the socio-economic scale, namely professional specialty/technical, executive/administrative/managerial, and business ownership. The major gender difference lies in the much lower proportion of women than men in the executive/administrative/managerial category (10.3 versus 21 percent) and in the business ownership category (15.5 versus 31.6 percent). On the other hand, there are slightly more women than men (31 versus 26.3 percent) in the professional specialty/technical category. Keeping in mind that 15.5 percent of the women in the sample are homemakers, we can regard the proportion of 56.8 percent of the female respondents in the top three categories as rather significant, especially since most of them are raising or have raised children.

Overall, my findings validate the picture of permanent French immigrants as successful individuals (men and women alike) who seem determined to make a place for themselves in American society from a socio-economic point of view. Particularly indicative of social integration is the high proportion of women in my sample (currently or previously) holding jobs, despite the fact that some could have chosen to stay at home and be supported by their spouses.

CITIZENSHIP STATUS

Another factor and predictor of acculturation, besides the parameters we just discussed, is citizenship status. It has been noted that "citizenship acquisition is the first stage for any foreign minority that wishes to make itself heard" (Portes and Rumbaut 1996: 115). Judging by this criterion, we can say that a sizable portion of the French population in the United States does not feel any pressing need to be heard. The 1990 U.S. Census reports a 52.6 percent rate of naturalization for the French living in this country. My data show a comparable rate of 54.2 percent, as indicated in Figure 4.4. Conversely, 45.8 percent of the respondents in my sample have remained exclusively French.

Within the category of naturalized individuals, some are exclusively U.S. citizens, while others are dual (French and American) nationals. These two subcategories are respectively represented by 33.3 and 20.8 percent of the respondents in my sample. These figures reflect the fact that, for a period of time beginning in the mid 1970s, there was no requirement to renounce French citizenship in order to acquire U.S. citizenship.

The distribution shown in Figure 4.4 reveals interesting gender differences. Over 60 percent of the female respondents are American citizens, versus fewer than 45 percent of the male respondents—a strong parallel to the 56.1 versus 47.2 percent gender distribution reported in the 1990 U.S. Census for the entire French population in the nation.

Figure 4.4
Citizenship Status by Gender

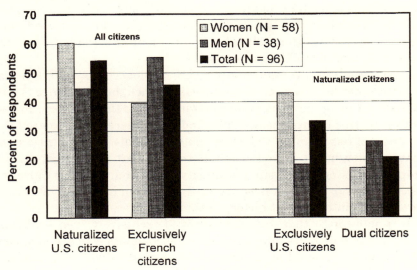

In addition, while 43 percent of the women are exclusively U.S. citizens and 17.2 percent dual nationals, the proportions are reversed in the case of men: only 18.5 percent are exclusively U.S. citizens, versus 26.3 percent dual nationals.

This gender distribution shows French women to be more willing than French men to acquire U.S. citizenship, even at the cost of renouncing their French citizenship if required to do so. Several of the male respondents indicated to me that they would never have changed their citizenship status if the previously mentioned "window of opportunity" had not allowed them to become U.S. citizens without renouncing their French citizenship.

Let us return to the 44 individuals in my sample who have remained exclusively French. How can we account for the fact that these 23 women (almost 40 percent of the female respondents) and 21 men (over 55 percent of the male respondents) have not acquired U.S. citizenship, thus forgoing the exercise of political rights in this country? Do they differ in significant ways from the rest of the sample? If so, what does it tell us about the acculturation process?

Two factors commonly related to change of citizenship status are length of residence in the host country and marital status. The first one is somewhat significant in the case at hand. As indicated earlier, the average length of U.S. residence is 27.2 years for all respondents in my sample. By contrast, it is 39 years for those who are exclusively U.S. citizens and 34.5 years for the dual nationals; however, the range is 19 to 74 years in the first case and 17 to 58 years in the second case, attesting to the fact that naturalization is a matter of individual choice for the French in the United States.

As expected, the average length of U.S. residence is lowest (18 years) for those who have remained exclusively French, but the range is 5 to 66 years. Among the 44 respondents who fall into this category, 25 had arrived in this country before 1980 and could therefore have used the "window of opportunity" to become dual nationals. Their decision not to do so must be attributed mostly to the fact that a change of citizenship status is not, for them, a necessity at the individual or collective level; there has been no need for political action on behalf of French immigrants in the recent history of this country.

It is noteworthy that this same set of 44 exclusively French citizens in my sample includes only 7 of the 28 respondents who are members of all-French couples. Except for 7 never-married individuals, all others are members of mixed couples in which the non-French spouse is either an American (27 cases) or another non-French national (3 cases), indicating that the marriage factor does not influence change of citizenship status as much as might have been expected.

Let us focus for a moment on the educational level of the 17 women and 10 men who are married to Americans and have not become U.S. citizens. Their educational levels show no consistent pattern, ranging as they do from eighth-grade to advanced degrees. However, a majority of them are at the upper end of the scale: 10 have an associate or bachelor's degree, 4 a master's degree, and 3 a doctoral degree. In keeping with their educational attainment, most of these respondents fall into the top three occupational categories represented in my sample: 10 of them are professionals, 5 are business owners, and 4 have managerial positions. It seems surprising that they would live as disenfranchised citizens in their country of residence for more than a few years. The naturalization process should certainly not be intimidating for such highly positioned individuals. A better explanation lies in their strong attachment to an element of their French identity that is obviously charged with symbolism.

This last point was brought to my attention by the comments of a highly educated and well-adjusted woman with deep roots in this country; her late husband was a career officer in the U.S. army, and she has U.S.-born children and grandchildren.

> I got my American citizenship a while back, when you did not have to renounce your French citizenship. It was about time, after living here for almost 50 years as a permanent resident. . . . But you know something, I still remain French, since I did not have to renounce my French citizenship, and I would never have wanted to do that, as much as I love the United States!

These remarks seem to reveal some deep-seated ambivalence about total integration into American society—at the price of being deprived of electoral rights and participation in the decision-making process at various levels. They serve to underline the fact that an immigrant's adaptation to a new society is conditioned by a number of factors that may not all converge.

In the case of the French population in the United States, one might have expected factors of acculturation such as demographic composition, outmarriage, and socio-economic integration to be associated with a higher naturalization rate than the one we have discovered. However, a number of other variables may intersect with these structural factors of acculturation, including purely personal considerations. For instance, the fact that the French tend to emigrate singly means that their families of origin in France may (explicitly or implicitly) exercise pressure on them to retain their French citizenship. The "return dream" can also be a factor, facilitated by the ease with which some French immigrants could find their place again in France. Finally, French people do not feel the need, generally speaking, to "prove themselves" by acquiring U.S. citizenship, since they are on the whole well accepted by Americans.

REPRISE

We have examined in this chapter a number of socio-demographic features that point to a high degree of acculturation in the current French population in the United States. Present-day French immigrants tend to reside among non-French people, and intermarriage is a common phenomenon, particularly in the case of women. Their level of educational attainment and occupational status tends to be high, in both women and men.

We might have expected the convergence of residence and marriage patterns with socio-economic position to translate into a perfect model of integration into American society. However, our consideration of citizenship status prevents us from concluding that permanent French immigrants totally blend into the American mainstream. We discovered that even some long-term residents with strong family ties in the United States have not acquired American citizenship, due in part to their persistent ties to a distant homeland. This fact alone serves to underline the appropriateness of the concept of acculturation, rather than assimilation: Successful adaptation to life in a new country does not necessarily preclude a certain degree of attachment to one's country of origin.

5

Life at Home and Beyond: Behavioral and Interactional Factors of Acculturation

Personal choice plays a particularly important role in ethnicity in the case of "white ethnics" who can easily blend into mainstream American society, as illustrated by the French immigrant population in the United States. While its socio-demographic characteristics point in the general direction of extensive adaptation, we discovered that some of its members stop short of total integration at the societal level by choosing not to acquire U.S. citizenship.

This seeming inconsistency reminds us that a complete picture of acculturation requires an examination, beyond the façade of public life, of the behavioral and interactional patterns that are distinctive of an immigrant population. How do its members live their private lives at home and beyond? What are their adaptive strategies? To what extent do their behavior and interaction fashion a collective identity marking them as a group within the context of American diversity?

These issues are especially worthy of consideration in the case of an immigrant population, such as the French in the United States, which remains fairly invisible on the American ethnic scene. I will address them on the basis of my ethnographic interviews, buttressed by many years of participant observation in French homes and circles that, owing to my insider status, have always been open to my scrutiny.

The primary source of data for the analysis to be presented in this chapter is the set of semiformal interviews that I collected in two of my three ethnographic sites: the metropolitan Los Angeles area and se-mirural southern Oregon. These settings, while being both located in the Pacific region, differ drastically in terms of ease of contact with the French world, and to a certain extent in levels of conformity to main-stream American culture, warranting a comparative study of strategies in ordinary everyday life. Each location is represented by a sample of 30 respondents consisting of 18 women and 12 men—in keeping with the two-thirds/one-third gender distribution in the French population at large in the United States.

It should be noted at the outset that French immigrants are in a special position in this country due to the reputation of their culture. "Frenchness has always been in America a 'most favored' foreign cul-ture. . . . French cooking, manners, fashions, music, books and plays, and for that matter the French language itself have always had a wide audience in the United States" (Higonnet 1980:386–87). Given this sit-uation, French immigrants can often count on Americans' tacit ap-proval, or even encouragement, of their attachment to the French national heritage. This point is well illustrated, on a minor scale, by remarks that are familiar to native speakers of French living in the United States: "Don't lose your French accent, it's just so nice/charm-ing/delightful/romantic."

However, the French are no exception to the "rule" that norms of behavior and interaction characteristic of American society have an impact on the way they conduct their lives, even out of the public eye. Our examination of their private lives at home and beyond makes use of key indicators of ethnicity, such as food patterns and organizational activities. We will show these behavioral and interactional factors of acculturation to be both causes and effects in the process of adaptation to American society.

LIFE AT HOME

The daily routine of immigrants' lives at home can be revealing of their adaptation to a new society. Food patterns, holiday celebrations, and use of the media are spheres of activity that lend themselves to the exercise of personal freedom, making them valuable indicators in a study of variable ethnicity.

Table 5.1
Food Patterns at Home (N = number of respondents)

	L.A. area (N = 30)	S. Oregon (N = 30)	Both locations (N = 60)
French dominant	8	6	14
U.S. dominant	0	3	3
Mixed	22	21	43

Food Patterns

A notable ingredient of the French culture is a passion for food. Commonly associated with it, among people who live in France, is a rather exalted view of French cuisine that is often accompanied by a biased opinion of American cuisine—based in part on stereotypes inspired by McDonald's and other fast food chains. Given this dimension of the national ethos, as well as the worldwide reputation of French cuisine, natives of France living in the United States might be expected to cling to their food traditions as much as possible. However, no such picture emerges from my investigation among first-generation French immigrants in the Pacific region, as shown in Table 5.1.

In response to my query about their food practices at home (Item #19 in the Appendix), only 14 respondents out of 60 report French dominant patterns, while 3 report U.S. dominant patterns; the remaining 43 fall into the "mixed" category, indicating a high degree of accommodative behavior in the sample at large.

The distribution differs only slightly in the two geographical locales. In each of them, a majority of the respondents reports mixed patterns, with almost identical numbers in the L.A. area (22) and S. Oregon (21). French dominant patterns are reported by 8 respondents in the L.A. area versus 6 in S. Oregon, and U.S. dominant patterns by none in the L.A. area versus 3 in S. Oregon.

While the figures go in the expected direction, with a slightly higher degree of native culture retention in the L.A. area, the differences between the two sets of respondents are too small to be regarded as significant. The absence of clear differences can be attributed in part to the increasing availability of French food items in many locations in the United States. It is now almost as easy in a small southern Oregon town as it is in a major urban area to buy ingredients for a French meal.

Interestingly, some of the respondents who report mixed food patterns at home feel compelled to rationalize their behavior.

> The reason we do not eat only the French way is that we are vegetarians, and French cuisine is not as well adapted to it as American cuisine.

> Sometimes we eat American food or couscous, just to get away from all the French food I have to cook every day at the restaurant.

Others give specifications that reveal a desire to mark a boundary between themselves and "mainstream" Americans regarding food patterns, as well as table manners.

> We eat mostly in a mixed way, but we *never* serve hamburgers or sodas in this house.

> When I say that we eat mostly the French way, I also mean that nobody may leave the table before the meal is over. That's one thing I am strict about.

Overall, however, my interview data confirm what I have observed for many years: French immigrants living in the Pacific region, regardless of the exact location, often use accommodative strategies in their food practices. I would characterize the general tendency as a case of benign adaptation to local mores—in the choice of foods as well as the organization of a meal—associated with a deep attachment to French cuisine that, however, finds expression in words more often than it does in actions.

Celebration of Holidays

A similar degree of acculturation appears to characterize the celebration of holidays by first-generation French immigrants. Participants in my study were asked whether they observe only French holidays, only American holidays, or both (Item #17 in the Appendix). Table 5.2 shows that 3 respondents observe only French holidays and 12 only American holidays, while 42 observe both—the litmus test being observance of Independence Day on July 4th and of Bastille Day on July 14th. The 3 remaining respondents report that they do not observe any holidays.

Table 5.2
Observance of French and American Holidays (N = number of respondents)

	L.A. area (N = 30)	S. Oregon (N = 30)	Both locations (N = 60)
Only French holidays	0	3	3
Only U.S. holidays	5	7	12
Both	22	20	42
Neither	3	0	3

There are only slight differences between the two samples of respondents. In each case, a majority observes both French and American holidays, with almost identical numbers in the L.A. area (22) and S. Oregon (20). The other respondents fall into the following categories: observance of only French holidays is reported by none in the L.A. area, versus 3 in S. Oregon; observance of only American holidays is reported by 5 in the L.A. area, versus 7 in S. Oregon; the 3 respondents who report no observance of holidays reside in the L.A. area.

Although the difference is hardly significant, it is somewhat surprising to find that the few respondents who observe only French holidays are all residents of Southern Oregon. One of them, a man who has lived in this country for over 30 years and is an American citizen, shows particularly strong determination in celebrating Bastille Day, but *not* July 4th. The French holiday is an occasion for him to display national paraphernalia and experience *esprit de corps* for one day.

> Every year we invite all of our French friends and their spouses to come for the day. We have French military music, French decorations and of course a French flag, and then we eat and drink and dance for hours, just like in France.

Bastille Day is by far the most popular of all French holidays observed by the respondents, many of whom do not keep up with the rest of the French calendar. Only a few have a larger inventory of traditions, which may include having *galette des Rois* (almond paste flat cake) for the Feast of Kings on January 6th (Epiphany), and making French crêpes on the exact day of Mardi-Gras just before Lent. As for those who observe only American holidays, they seem to regard Thanksgiving as an extremely important day; but even this particular holiday, which

Table 5.3
Celebration of Common Holidays (N = number of respondents)

	L.A. area (N = 30)	S. Oregon (N = 30)	Both locations (N = 60)
French patterns	6	2	8
American patterns	2	11	13
Mixed patterns	19	17	36
Do not celebrate holidays	3	0	3

is unknown in France, can be the occasion for celebrations with a French flavor.

> At Thanksgiving my [American] husband and I never have turkey. We just go to the beach with a bunch of American and French friends and we have a picnic with French bread, pâté and champagne.

Participants in my study were also asked to indicate how they celebrate holidays that are common to both countries, such as Christmas (Item #18 in the Appendix). Table 5.3 shows 8 of them reporting French patterns. Among the remaining 49 respondents who observe such holidays, 13 celebrate the American way and 36 have mixed patterns.

The figures are very similar in the two geographical locations for those who report mixed patterns: 19 in the L.A. area, 17 in S. Oregon. However, among the 21 respondents who observe these common holidays, we find inverse proportions of those who celebrate the French way (6 in the L.A. area versus 2 in S. Oregon), and those who celebrate the American way (2 in the L.A. area versus 11 in S. Oregon). These differences can, of course, be attributed in part to more limited resources in the semirural setting; but another factor that occasionally enters into play is the pressure of local norms, due to the lack of cultural diversity.

> It is not always easy to observe French traditions in our home here in Oregon, especially at Christmas time. Our children resent having to wait till Christmas Eve to display the presents, they always say: "Why do we have to be different from the neighbors?" So sometimes we just give in.

All in all, the frequent occurrence of mixed patterns for the celebration of holidays common to France and the United States, coupled with the preponderance of observance of both French and American holidays as just discussed, shows the participants in this study to use accommodative strategies: They adapt a great deal to American life in this regard but do not necessarily forget their native traditions. As in the case of food practices, my participant observation over the years confirms these findings. First-generation French immigrants most often regard American holidays and patterns of celebration as a positive addition to their cultural inventory, rather than an erasure of their French heritage.

Use of the Media

Three sources of contact with the French world are examined here: radio, television, and periodicals. Had my fieldwork been conducted a few years later than it was (mid-1990s), I would have included the Internet. But at the time, home computers and especially access to the Internet were not as widespread as they are today, giving more importance to other media for keeping in touch with the French world.

The role of radio, however, was already largely insignificant, and it will most likely continue to diminish, due in particular to the spread of cable television. When I asked participants in my study whether or not they listen to French radio programs, some of them looked at me in disbelief and inquired: "Which ones?" In Los Angeles, I could at least inform them of the existence of a locally produced French program devoted to cultural matters, which aired every Saturday morning. But no such programs existed in southern Oregon, and few people wanted to depend on short wave radio to remain in contact with France. One respondent reported doing so but lamented the difficulty of scheduling listening times, given the nine-hour time difference between the West Coast and France.

As indicated in Table 5.4, only 7 L.A. area respondents, and none in S. Oregon, report occasionally listening to French radio programs. On the other hand, both sets of respondents make use of television to keep in touch with France: 42 of the 60 respondents (approximately two-thirds) watch French programs either frequently (9) or sometimes (33). Some slight differences emerge between the two sets of respondents:

Table 5.4
Use of French-Language Media (N = number of respondents)

	L.A. area (N = 30)	S. Oregon (N = 30)	Both locations (N = 60)
Radio			
Frequently	0	0	0
Sometimes	7	0	7
Never	23	30	53
Television			
Frequently	5	4	9
Sometimes	18	15	33
Never	7	11	18
Written press			
Frequently	18	6	24
Sometimes	12	21	33
Never	0	3	3

23 of them in the L.A. area watch French television programs either frequently (5) or sometimes (18), while 7 never do; 19 in S. Oregon watch them either frequently (4) or sometimes (15), while 11 never do. The nonwatchers in S. Oregon complain about their inability to access French programs without an expensive subscription to cable television—a problem that does not arise in the L.A. area, where such programs appear on a regular channel.

The respondents' favorite types of programs are identical in the two locations. Daily newscasts directly transmitted from Paris come in first place, closely followed by films and plays (some of them transmitted live from theaters in France), and game shows as a distant third. The predilection for newscasts indicates that natives of France retain at least a passive passion for politics—a subject of great daily interest in their homeland.

> The newscasts from Paris provide so much information about world events, and then we get the French perspective on them. And of course, I also love to keep up with French politics and many other kinds of events in France.

Given such preoccupations in first-generation French immigrants, it is not surprising that they are avid consumers of French periodicals produced either in France or, less often, in the United States. Table 5.4

shows that, among the 60 respondents under consideration, 57 read French-language magazines or newspapers frequently (24) or sometimes (33). But the level of frequency varies widely from one geographical location to the other. The L.A. area sample has 18 frequent and 12 occasional readers of French periodicals; the S. Oregon sample has 6 frequent and 21 occasional readers, plus 3 respondents who never read any French periodicals.

Obviously, the degree of accessibility of such reading material, in stores or in libraries, is much higher in a major urban center than it is in a semirural area. However, this practical consideration does not fully account for the different reading habits of the two groups, since subscriptions are readily available for all the periodicals in question. Let us briefly examine the nature of the reading material in each location.

The periodical most often listed by L.A. area respondents is the daily or weekly *Le Monde*, a highly regarded austere newspaper dealing with important political, social, and intellectual/artistic issues. By contrast, the periodical most often listed by S. Oregon respondents is *Paris-Match*, a rather superficial weekly magazine in which much space is devoted to photography. Other periodicals often listed by L.A. area respondents are *L'Express* and *Le Point*, two rather comprehensive weeklies, and the U.S.-based monthlies *Journal Français* and *France-Amérique*. These last four publications have fewer readers in the S. Oregon sample, which on the other hand has more readership of specialized magazines (arts, crafts, etc.) and the feminine press (e.g., *Elle*, *Marie-Claire*). So we can say that this particular set of readers shows more interest in specific topics than it does in general French culture or French perspectives on world events. This fact, combined with the reading frequencies indicated earlier, points to a lower degree of native culture retention in the semirural setting, as compared with the urban setting.

Overall, however, it is clear that many first-generation immigrants from France remain in contact with their culture of origin through their use of the French media, particularly the written press. This last feature seems congruent with their educational attainment, as well as the high regard in which reading is held in their homeland—a characteristic that has been noted by American observers of present-day French society such as Platt (1995).

REPRISE

Our examination of French immigrants' lives at home has uncovered a high degree of adaptation to American food patterns and holiday celebrations. However, it often co-exists with the maintenance of some French customs and traditions. Native culture retention is also achieved through an abundant use of the French media, especially the written press.

The significance of geographic location has not really been proven. We found a somewhat higher level of retention of the French culture in the urban setting, particularly regarding the celebration of holidays common to both countries, as well as the use of French-language periodicals. But we also noted that certain French traditions, such as the celebration of Bastille Day, are particularly strongly maintained by some natives of France who live as "isolates" in semirural southern Oregon—which points to the important role of personal choice in behavioral manifestations of ethnicity.

LIFE BEYOND HOME

French immigrants in the United States have the reputation of not being particularly gregarious among themselves. This characteristic has been attributed in part to the "notoriously low capacity for group action" of French people in general (Higonnet 1980: 385), a comment that finds an echo in some of my respondents' remarks.

> I'm just not a joiner, that's the French way.

> Maybe because of the traditional French individualism of non-involvement with any group, French people rarely participate in anything French in this country, so they lose their identity in the melting-pot.

To what extent does the last statement correspond to the reality? The issue of collective identity for an immigrant population is closely linked to organizational activities in the community, informal friendship and acquaintance networks in the host country, and visits to the homeland. We will deal in turn with these three aspects of the lives of French immigrants in the United States.

This part of my analysis owes a great deal to a sociological study in which the "Armenian-American subculture" is regarded as consisting of "both the formally organized structure of voluntary associations and the activities they produce and the informal networks of friends and acquaintances" (Bakalian 1993: 179). I also consider visits to the homeland because they constitute an important strategy for native culture retention in the case of the French.

In contrast with Bakalian's work, which contains an extensive analysis of the role of church and politics in the lives of Armenian Americans, this study barely touches on such institutions, since they presently have little significance in the lives of French immigrants. As indicated earlier, the French do not sense a need for group-oriented political action in this country, given their position in American society. Likewise, they lack strong ties among themselves through church, due to their low level of affiliation with Roman Catholicism, the most common religion in their homeland, or with any other religion.

The few existing French Catholic parishes in the United States appear to be in decline. A case in point is the current situation at the Church of Notre Dame des Victoires in San Francisco, a landmark in an area that was once a thriving French neighborhood. Father Siffert, who heads the parish, describes today's parishioners as aging French immigrants or people other than French who live in the proximity, including some Chinese Catholics from nearby Chinatown (personal communication, February 1999). Given this mixed audience, most religious services are now conducted in English, and the French language is also losing ground at the parochial school attached to the church. This situation results in part from the transformation of a residential neighborhood into a business area. The French who used to live close to the church and school now reside in other parts of town or in the suburbs, and those who wish to attend Catholic services may do so in other churches, rather than drive a long way to the national parish.

The fate of Notre Dame des Victoires also reflects the current attitude of French people in general toward religion. France has witnessed a drastic decline in church attendance in the last few decades, a trend that social analysts commonly attribute to the failure of the French Catholic church to keep pace with evolving mores and values, particularly in the area of marriage and the family. The French, being independently minded, have turned to other value systems that are better adapted to the circumstances of modern life, notwithstanding their high degree of cultural identification with Catholicism due to the history and traditions of France. Official figures for the late 1990s indicate that approximately 81 percent of the people living in France still regard themselves as Catholics, the remainder being approximately 7 percent Muslim, 1.7 percent Protestant, 1.3 percent Jewish, and 9 percent other. However, only a fraction (at the most one-fourth) of self-labeled Catholics actually attends church on a regular or even occasional basis.

Many of the respondents in my sample were raised in France at a time when the nation was still over 90 percent Catholic (before the gradual spread of the Muslim religion in the last three decades due mainly to immigration from North Africa) and church attendance was still high. In view of this situation, it seemed superfluous to include in my semiformal interview any direct question about religious affiliation, an area of life that the French consider as highly private. As I expected, a number of facts regarding the respondents' current religious practices (or lack of) came to light anyway, usually in the form of volunteered comments such as "I was raised as a Catholic but. . . ." Only a few of the participants in my study gave me evidence of having kept up with the Catholic religion in this country, which concurs with my own observations over the years. It also concurs with the results of a recent survey of religious practices in various U.S. immigrant populations, according to which people of French origin have one of the lowest rates of identification with their "old-country religion" (Hammond and Warner 1993).

An important contributing factor probably is the high intermarriage rate reported earlier for French immigrants, even in the foreign-born generation. A significant number of respondents in my sample have non-Catholic spouses, most often Protestant or Jewish. It is beyond the scope of this study to reconstruct the causal chain for French immigrants in the United States: Is their overall lack of interest in the Catholic church (and often religion in general) a consequence of outmarriage? Or did some self-selection process operate, making those who already had weaker ties with the Catholic church more likely candidates for emigration and outmarriage? The second hypothesis seems more valid, since even a few mononational (French) couples in my sample have not maintained their native Catholicism, turning to other religions or most often not practicing any.

I will briefly return to the subject of church and politics when discussing participation in voluntary associations and community activities, but it should be clear by now that religion can hardly be considered as a bond between French immigrants in the United States. As for school, another formal institution that can play a major role in creating and maintaining a collective identity in an immigrant population, it will also be the subject of mere passing remarks (in Chapter 7), since few contemporary French immigrants send their children to French or bilingual schools in the United States.

In the quasi-absence of strong ties through church, school, or politics within their ranks, can French immigrants in the United States be considered as a distinctive group on the American ethnic scene? To what extent do they conduct their lives in ways that enable them not only to retain elements of their native culture, but also to establish group boundaries between themselves and others? Our discussion begins with an examination of formal ties with the community. As in the first part of this chapter, we compare behavioral and interactional patterns in two geographical locations (the L.A. area and S. Oregon) that differ greatly in accessibility to French community resources. We also highlight again the significance of personal choice in the lives of French immigrants in this country.

Formal Ties with the Community

The analysis presented in this section is primarily based on the respondents' answers to several questions (Items #46–51 in the Appendix) dealing with their degree of involvement in French and non-French organizational activities, as well as any French-oriented public actions which they may have taken. Following Bakalian (1993), I facilitated the respondents' task in answering some of the structured questions by presenting them with a list of types of voluntary association and an inventory of community activities; other structured questions dealt with frequency of participation. The inventories appearing in the interview guide (Item #46 in the Appendix) have been slightly reorganized here for the sake of simplicity. I have grouped together three types of voluntary association (professional, scholarly, and student organizations) that, at a general level, have a common goal of furthering knowledge. Also, the expression "non-French association" has been changed to "American association," since none of the respondents made any specific mention of associations other than French or American.

The general picture emerging from the data, as shown in Tables 5.5 and 5.6, is one of low and selective involvement in both French and American voluntary associations. First of all, 21 of the 60 respondents (over one-third of the sample) do not belong to any such organization,

Table 5.5
Membership in French Voluntary Associations (N = 30 cases, in rank order of multiple responses)

	L.A. area	S. Oregon	Both locations
Cultural organization	7	9	16
Prof/scholarly/student association	5	1	6
Compatriotic society	5	0	5
Choir/dance group	0	2	2
Sports organization	1	0	1
Church committee	0	0	0
Charitable organization	0	0	0
Political organization	0	0	0

and for the 39 respondents who do, the number of cases of membership averages approximately two per individual. Second, the 81 cases of membership in French and American voluntary associations do not spread evenly over the whole spectrum: They amount to 29 in professional/scholarly/student organizations, 21 in cultural organizations, 8 in church committees, 7 in charitable organizations, 7 in sports organizations, 6 in compatriotic societies, 3 in choirs/dance groups, and none in political organizations. This general picture shows participants in my study to be drawn mainly to associations that are linked to their occupational status or individual concerns rather than collective interests.

Tables 5.5 and 5.6 also indicate that cases of membership in French voluntary associations are clearly outnumbered by those in American associations: 30 versus 51. At the top of the list on the French side (Table 5.5) are cultural organizations (16 cases), followed by professional/scholarly/student associations as a distant second (6 cases), compatriotic societies (5 cases), choirs/dance groups (2 cases), and sports organizations (1 case). The glaring absence of membership in French church committees, charitable organizations, or political organizations points to a lack of commitment in those areas.

At the top of the list on the American side (Table 5.6) are professional/scholarly/student associations (23 cases), followed by church committees as a distant second (8 cases), charitable organizations (7 cases), sports organizations (6 cases), cultural organizations (5 cases), compatriotic societies (1 case), and choirs/dance groups (1 case). There are no cases of membership in political organizations, evidencing a lack of

Table 5.6
Membership in American Voluntary Associations (N = 51 cases, in rank order of multiple responses)

	L.A. area	S. Oregon	Both locations
Prof/scholarly/student association	13	10	23
Church committee	2	6	8
Charitable organization	3	4	7
Sports organization	2	4	6
Cultural organization	2	3	5
Compatriotic society	1	0	1
Choir/dance group	0	1	1
Political organization	0	0	0

active involvement in U.S. politics, which corresponds to my earlier comments regarding resistance to naturalization in some of the respondents.

The difference between the French and American inventories is particularly marked in two areas. Membership in professional/scholarly/student associations is much less frequent on the French side (6 cases) than it is on the American side (23 cases), which should not come as a surprise, given the limited availability of French associations of this type in the United States. But the proportions are reversed for cultural organizations: There are 16 cases of membership on the French side, versus only 5 on the American side, despite the much greater availability of the latter. This distribution points to an interesting combination, in French immigrants, of occupational integration into American society on the one hand, and on the other hand, a desire in some of them to remain in contact with their culture of origin through affiliation in French cultural organizations.

By contrast, the respondents' low degree of involvement in church committees confirms my earlier picture of the minimal place of religion in the lives of French immigrants in the United States. It is rather significant that only two of the eight individuals listing memberships in (American) church committees are affiliated with the Catholic religion. The others divide as follows: three in various Protestant churches (Lutheran, Mormon, Evangelical), two in nondenominational Christian churches, and one in a Buddhist temple.

My interview data also show that few respondents had held a position of responsibility in some organization during the previous year (Item

#47 in the Appendix): one did in a French cultural association and five in American associations of various types. As for simple attendance at meetings of French organizations, with or without membership and specific responsibilities (Item #48 in the Appendix), its level of frequency is rather low: One-third of the respondents sometimes or frequently attend such meetings, while two-thirds rarely or never do so.

Participation in the previous year in community activities sponsored by French organizations (Item #49 in the Appendix) has a better record than meetings: 35 of the 60 respondents answered positively when presented with a list of ten different types of event (adapted from Bakalian 1993). Most frequently attended are French-sponsored parties: Such attendance in the 12 previous months was reported by 16 respondents, in most cases more than once or twice, and in one case more than six times. However, these figures must be handled with care, since several of the individuals concerned have a professional obligation to attend such events (cocktail parties in particular) on a regular basis. The same can be said about a few of the 15 respondents who, during the previous year, had attended official Bastille Day celebrations—not to be confused with the kind of private celebration we depicted earlier.

The figures reflecting attendance at other types of French-sponsored activities in the 12 previous months indicate a marked preference for events of an intellectual or artistic nature: 16 respondents had attended lectures/panel discussions either once or twice (11 cases) or more frequently (5 cases); the following types of events had been attended once or twice: concerts (10 respondents), art exhibits (9 respondents), theater (5 respondents), dance shows (2 respondents), and French film presentations (2 respondents). Picnics were listed by seven respondents, most of whom had attended once or twice, and bazaars by three respondents who had attended once or twice.

Respondents were also asked to give a general idea of their frequency of attendance at community events sponsored by non-French organizations (Item #50 in the Appendix). Only 26 of the 60 respondents sometimes or frequently attend such events, and 34 never or rarely do so. While the record was slightly better for French-sponsored community activities, as previously reported, we are forced to conclude that French immigrants have a relatively low degree of involvement in community life.

Such a conclusion is in keeping with my respondents' degree and kind of involvement in public actions related to the French population in the

United States (Item #51 in the Appendix). One-third of the respondents report that they have never taken any such action. Other responses fall into the following categories, in ascending order of frequency: 8 responses regarding help in establishing a French school; 15 responses regarding help in locating jobs for French people; 18 responses regarding the furthering of French interests in the community through volunteer activities such as lecturing about France, leading a French conversation group, or working on a sister-city project; 21 responses regarding other types of actions, such as regular volunteering as a French language tutor or occasional volunteering as a translator. With the exception of the first type (help in establishing a French school), these actions, while laudable, do not translate into the creation and maintenance of a collective identity among French immigrants in the United States.

The findings presented in this section indicate that French immigrants, when making efforts to remain in touch with their origins through formal ties with community, tend to do it mainly through participation in organizations and activities of an intellectual or artistic nature. Are such efforts sufficient to create a sense of solidarity and commonness of purpose, resulting in the creation and maintenance of group boundaries? The answer probably has to be negative, particularly in view of the high proportion of individuals who are not involved in any French organizations or French-sponsored community activities. Obviously, many present-day French immigrants in the United States do not feel any particular urge to do so, even when the opportunities are there, because such involvement is a matter of choice rather than a necessity.

This last point is made especially clear by a comparison of the "activity record" of respondents in the L.A. area and in S. Oregon. Their degree of community involvement through formal ties does not differ much, despite the enormous difference in availability of resources between the two geographical locales; moreover, when it differs, the figures do not always go in the expected direction. Let us summarize some of the findings, most of which are presented in Tables 5.5 and 5.6:

- The number of respondents who are members of (French or American) voluntary associations is, surprisingly, even lower in the L.A. area (18 out of 30) than it is in S. Oregon (21 out of 30).

- Equally surprising, the total number of cases of membership in French and American organizations is almost identical in the two locations: 41 in the L.A. area, 40 in S. Oregon.

- The higher number of cases of membership in French organizations in the L.A. area (18, versus 12 in S. Oregon) is due mainly to more frequent involvement in two types of associations that are less accessible, if at all, in the second location: professional/scholarly/student organizations (5 cases, versus 1 in S. Oregon) and compatriotic societies (5 cases, versus none in S. Oregon).

- The lower number of cases of membership in American voluntary associations in the L.A. area (23 versus 28 in S. Oregon) is due mainly to less frequent involvement in church committees (2 cases, versus 6 in S. Oregon).

It would be of little interest to compare the two samples of respondents for some of the other activities listed above (e.g., French art exhibits), since the semirural setting offers practically no such opportunities. Suffice it to say that, as expected, the L.A. area respondents report higher frequency of attendance at such events (French-sponsored or not) than the S. Oregon respondents.

Let us now turn to the reasons evoked by some respondents for their low degree of involvement in organizational and community life (Items #48–50 in the Appendix). The two samples do not differ in any significant way in this respect. Lack of time and/or money is by the far the most frequently cited reason in both locations, with a number of respondents emphasizing the time factor, including some who are retired. Personal preference comes next, with numerous respondents stating that they are not "joiners" and others blaming co-ethnics for their own behavior.

> I would like to participate in French activities, but I think that French people are very critical, and I choose not to be around that kind of person.

Surprisingly, the lack of opportunities is mentioned as another reason not only by S. Oregon respondents, but also by several L.A. area residents, who profess to be unaware of the availability of numerous French-sponsored events within a reasonable distance. Finally, other reasons such as health or transportation problems, as well as work schedule, are given by a number of respondents who occasionally use them as excuses. Such is the case of a S. Oregon respondent who, after emphatically pointing to her nondriver status, later revealed that her sons can give her a ride "whenever and wherever" she wants to go.

Overall, first-generation French immigrants appear to be only mildly interested, regardless of geographical location, in formal ties with the community that would help them to remain in touch with their origins. This is in keeping with the respondents' answers to a general question formulated as follows: How important do you think it is for you to participate in French activities and organizations in the United States? (Item #72 in the Appendix). Only 15 of the 60 respondents (one-fourth) regard it as very important; 23 regard it as somewhat important, despite their own lack of participation in a number of cases, and 8 as not important at all.

For those who regard such participation as very important, fulfillment of individual needs appears to play as much a part as the desire to preserve the French heritage.

> It [participation in French activities and organizations] makes you stronger, it gives you a sense of belonging, of identity and pride, and these are traits that can then be passed on to your children to make them better persons.

Another respondent's comment evidences a preference for organizations whose main function is to establish a bridge between the French and Americans, rather than create a sense of "in-groupness" in the French population in the United States.

> Participation in French organizations is important, but it has to be *positive*, for instance membership in the Alliance Française, *not* in separatist organizations.

Should we conclude that the French distaste for group action is entirely responsible for the absence of a collective identity among French immigrants in America? Before reaching such a conclusion, we need to examine their use of informal networks that can also play a role in the formation of ethnic identity.

Table 5.7
Three Closest Friends in USA (N = number of respondents)

	L.A. area (N = 30)	S. Oregon (N = 30)	Both locations (N = 60)
Three are French	2	5	7
Two are French	5	4	9
One is French	12	8	20
None is French	11	13	24

Informal Friendship and Acquaintance Networks

Two questions in my semiformal interviews addressed the issue of friendship networks. Respondents were asked to indicate the ethnicity of their three closest friends in the United States (Item #14 in the Appendix). They also had to provide information on the proportion of French individuals among their other friends in the United States (Item #15 in the Appendix).

Table 5.7 shows co-ethnic ties to be rather weak in terms of close friendship: Only 7 respondents report that all three of their closest friends in the United States are French, 9 report that two are French, 20 that one is French, and 24 that none is French. These figures add up to 59 French individuals among the respondents' three closest friends in the United States, which is only approximately one-third of the total possible number (180) for the 60 respondents. The proportion of French individuals among the respondents' other friends in the United States also reveals weak co-ethnic ties: Approximately one-third of the respondents report that it is "half or more"; for others it is "zero to less than half."

The L.A. sample shows a slightly lower proportion of French closest friends (31 percent) than the S. Oregon sample (34.5 percent). But the proportion of French people among the respondents' other friends in the United States is much higher in the L.A. area: 43 percent of the respondents, versus 20 percent in S. Oregon, report that "half or more" of their other friends in the United States are French, which suggests an overall higher use of co-ethnic friendship networks in the urban environment.

This picture is reinforced by a comparison of the two locations in terms of acquaintance networks. Interview questions focused on two specific issues. Respondents were asked whether they deal with French

Table 5.8
French Business Acquaintances in USA (N = number of respondents)

	L.A. area (N = 30)	S. Oregon (N = 30)	Both locations (N = 60)
Acquainted with only French professionals	3	1	4
Acquainted with only French businesses	7	9	16
Acquainted with both	6	1	7
Total	16	11	27

professionals in the United States and, if so, what types of professionals (Item #52 in the Appendix). They also had to indicate whether they patronize other French places of business mostly because of their co-ethnic nature and, if so, what kinds of business (Item #53 in the Appendix). Given the much greater availability of such resources in an urban setting, we can reasonably expect residents of the L.A. area to make much higher use of them than residents of S. Oregon—an assumption borne out by the data.

Table 5.8 indicates that almost half of all respondents in both locations (27 out of 60) make use of the services of French professionals and/or small businesses. But the proportion is lower in S. Oregon, with only 11 of the 30 respondents being acquainted with either French professionals (1) or French small businesses (9) or both (1). The only two professionals mentioned are a French accountant and a French physician. No multiple responses were offered by any of the 10 respondents who patronize French small businesses; in other words, none of them reports using several of these places of business. The range of establishments is rather limited: five respondents patronize a French restaurant, four patronize a car repair shop co-owned by a French man, and one patronizes a drapery store owned by a French woman.

In the L.A. area, on the other hand, 16 of the 30 respondents are acquainted with either French professionals (3) or French small businesses (7) or both (6), and there are numerous multiple responses. In other words, the 16 respondents often mention more than one type of professional and/or more than one type of small business, and they may patronize more than one establishment in a particular category, for instance, several restaurants or several grocery stores.

The French professionals listed by nine L.A. area respondents fall into six categories: physician, accountant, lawyer, dentist, business manager, engineer. The first of these categories (physician) is mentioned by four respondents, the second (accountant) by two, and the other categories by one each.

The French places of business patronized by 13 L.A.-area residents fall into eight different categories, with many of the respondents mentioning more than one category and/or more than one establishment within a certain category. The following list will give an idea of the range of French small businesses concerned. They are listed in descending order of number of responses, as indicated in parentheses next to the type of business: restaurant or café (8); wine or grocery store, bakery (7); bookstore (4); clothing or fashion store (3); antiques store (1); beauty shop (1); real estate office (1); specialized trading company (1); travel agency (1); video store (1).

It should not come as a surprise that establishments catering to French tastes for food and beverages are at the top of the list in both locations. In fact, one might have expected more respondents to mention such establishments, especially in the Los Angeles area where they are abundant. But it should be kept in mind that a number of French products are becoming more and more easily available even in chain stores, making it possible for French people, even in semirural Southern Oregon, to satisfy their needs for native food without necessarily patronizing a French establishment.

As for the other types of establishments listed for the Los Angeles area, their absence in semirural southern Oregon is deplored by a few of the respondents, who say they would probably patronize such places of business if they existed. The same situation prevails regarding the small number of French professionals in the area.

> When I lived in Los Angeles I had a French doctor, and when we moved to Bakersfield I found another. Here I've looked, but I still don't know of any nearby.

Others, however, seem rather content with the present situation, apparently not missing French professionals or French places of business very much. One respondent, when asked if she ever deals with French professionals, snapped back: "I never met one, and I would not be attracted." Since it had been her own decision to move to southern Oregon after becoming a widow, we have to assume that having a network of French acquaintances is indeed not a primary concern for her.

Table 5.9
Visits to the Homeland (N = number of respondents)

	L.A. area (N = 30)	S. Oregon (N = 30)	Both locations (N = 60)
Frequently	23	12	35
Sometimes	6	14	20
Never	1	4	5

Our examination of friendship and acquaintance networks shows first-generation French immigrants to make limited use of these informal social networks, regardless of geographical location. While French immigrants living in the Los Angeles area have more contacts with co-ethnics through such networks than those who live in semi-rural southern Oregon, the difference is not as great as might have been expected because residents of the L.A. area often by-pass available opportunities.

Visits to the Homeland

One way for immigrants to remain in touch with their native culture, in the absence of frequent interaction with co-ethnics in their country of residence, is to visit the homeland as often as possible. Natives of France might be expected to do so on a regular basis. Many of them still have close relatives and friends there and can afford to make the trip once in a while. Other considerations are the attractive nature of a trip to France, as well as the West European habit of taking long vacations.

In answer to my question about the frequency of their visits to the homeland (Item #20 in the Appendix), over half (35) of the 60 respondents report that they go frequently, that is, at least every two or three years; another third (20) report going sometimes, and only 5 never go (see Table 5.9). The most common pattern for those visits is a prolonged stay during the summer, giving first-generation immigrants' children the opportunity to get acquainted with French people and their French heritage. When asked to spell out their reasons for going to France (Item #63 in the Appendix), an overwhelming majority of the respondents list visiting relatives and friends as a primary goal, which means that they keep in close touch with French people and the French way of life.

Table 5.9 indicates that French immigrants living in the Los Angeles area have a particularly high frequency rate of visits to the homeland:

Most of them (23) go frequently, from several times a year to every two or three years; 6 go every four to nine years, and only 1 individual never goes. Some of these proportions are reversed in the case of the southern Oregon respondents: fewer than half (12) go frequently, from once a year to every two to three years; 14 go sometimes, with a range of four years to several decades between visits, and 4 never go.

There are several possible explanations for the differences between the two samples of respondents. First of all, in terms of logistics and transportation costs, it is much easier to plan a trip to France from the Los Angeles area than it is from southern Oregon. Second, people who live in an ethnically diverse setting often have exposure to other foreign-born individuals, some of whom regard regular visits to the homeland as an integral part of their lives. By contrast, people who reside in semirural southern Oregon are more prone to adopt the common American pattern of mini-vacations, rather than the French pattern of extended summer vacations.

But behind the curtain of practicalities or local social pressures, we find personal choice lurking again as a major determinant. Most first-generation French immigrants wishing to visit France could probably do so, at least on an occasional basis. Some of them, however, give evidence of a lack of steady interest in their homeland.

> I came to the United States in 1965 at age 18. At first I had no desire to make visits to France, but in 1990 I led a group of students on a summer tour. It gave me the idea to take my family there for a summer visit three years later.

> After coming to the United States in 1962 I never went back to France for many years, but in 1981 I decided to take one of my teenage grandsons there, and he liked it so much that we did it again in 1983 and 1985. I haven't gone back since, he is grown up and gone now.

In each of these two cases, a French-born individual finally decides to visit the homeland, not so much because of a burning desire to do so, but rather to accommodate other people. A few S. Oregon respondents go as far as showing distaste for visits to the homeland.

> I came to the United States in 1948 and went back to France for the first and only time in 1960 to see relatives and friends. I was shocked to find out that there was an anti-American attitude there, so I've never really wanted to go again.

While things have changed for the better in this respect in the last few years, it is not uncommon for French immigrants to encounter some expression of anti-Americanism when they visit their homeland, as if they were personally responsible for political or other actions by the American government or people. But it does not deter most French immigrants from visiting their country of origin, where they are usually made to feel at home again during their visit.

REPRISE

Our examination in this chapter of French immigrants' lives at home and beyond has uncovered a complex picture of acculturation. Their adaptation to American society is extensive in a number of ways, but we also found evidence of efforts on their part to remain in touch with their culture of origin. Two strategies stand out as major forces in this endeavor: use of the media, especially the French written press; and visits to the homeland. Each of them plays a significant role in native culture retention, and the second is particularly instrumental in the transmission of the French heritage, since children usually accompany their parents on their trips to France.

On the other hand, we found little evidence of strong ties or frequent social interaction within the French population in the United States. First-generation immigrants make only limited attempts to have regular contacts with one another, either through formal ties with the community or through informal friendship and acquaintance networks. These behavioral and interactional patterns are not conducive to group cohesiveness and solidarity and, therefore, produce no clear group boundaries between the French and others in the United States.

The variable nature of ethnicity in French immigrants was highlighted through a comparison of their lifestyles in two different geographical locations, namely the metropolitan Los Angeles area and semirural southern Oregon. Not surprisingly, we uncovered some distinctive locational patterns. The level of French culture retention was found to be higher in the urban setting, particularly regarding the use of French media, participation in French organizations and activities, informal acquaintance networks, and visits to the homeland. But there were also some unexpected findings: Individuals residing in the metropolitan Los Angeles area, even more so than those who live in semirural southern Oregon, often "by-pass" existing opportunities for

6

Perceptual Dimensions of Ethnicity

Beneath the array of socio-demographic, behavioral, and interactional features characterizing an immigrant population lies the more subjective realm of ethnicity. How do foreign-born individuals perceive themselves and their place in the host society? What are their mental representations of each component of their dual world? To what extent do these perceptions stand the test of reality? I address these issues in this chapter, delving into the actors' own perspectives on their situation, in an effort to go beyond a simple inventory of objective traits for an account of French ethnicity in the United States.

This part of my analysis is based on abundant material from the 96 semiformal interviews included in the final sample. Since the nature of the data varies a great deal, from labels for self-reference to inventories of personal likes and dislikes, methods of analysis are described in separate sections of this chapter, as they become relevant to my argument. Throughout the discussion, the focus is on the maintenance of a French identity in first-generation French immigrants, as attested by the data.

Table 6.1
Self-Labeling in Relation to Length of Residence in USA (N = 96 respondents)

	French %	French Am. %	American %	Other %
Under 10 yrs (N = 11)	63.6	27.2	9.0	0.0
10-25 yrs (N = 31)	25.8	48.3	9.6	16.1
Over 25 yrs (N = 54)	25.9	53.7	12.9	7.4
Total (N = 96)	30.1	49.0	11.5	9.4

SUBJECTIVE IDENTITY

Proponents of symbolic ethnicity emphasize the role of social actors in the "construction, destruction and reconstruction of ethnic attachments and identities" (Kivisto 1989: 16). If we accept the idea that the individuals concerned hold center stage in these processes, we need to consider subjective dimensions of ethnicity. Self-ascription, which does not necessarily correspond to ascription by others, can be explored through an examination of labels used for self-reference, as well as people's (often variable) self-identification in relation to their society of origin and their adoptive society.

Self-Labeling

The labels used by members of an immigrant population to refer to themselves can serve as preliminary indicators of subjective identity. In order to tap this source of information, I asked participants in my study to answer a question worded as follows (Item #11 in the Appendix): "Which of these labels best characterizes the way you consider yourself at the present time? American, French, French American, Other (Specify)."

Table 6.1 indicates that an overwhelming majority of the respondents refer to themselves as either "French" (30.1 percent) or "French American" (49 percent); only 11.5 percent refer to themselves as simply "American." The remaining 9.4 percent use other labels such as "citizen of the world."

Interestingly, approximately one-third of the 29 respondents who favor the label "French" for self-reference have acquired U.S. citizenship, which highlights the difference between psychological adjustment and socio-political adaptation to a host country. Conversely, 4 of the 11 respondents who label themselves as "American" have not acquired U.S. citizenship.

It should also be noted that these self-ascribed ethnic labels do not necessarily correlate with length of residence in the United States. As indicated in Table 6.1, the percentage of respondents who refer to themselves as "French" is expectedly highest (63.6 percent) among those who have been in this country under 10 years. But there is practically no difference between the two other sets of respondents: 25.8 percent of those with 10 to 25 years of U.S. residence call themselves "French" and so do 25.9 percent of those with more than 25 years.

Members of the last set occasionally express embarrassment about calling themselves French, after so many years in this country. "I came here 29 years ago and I'm a dual citizen, so maybe I should call myself an American. But honestly, I feel very French. However, I always remind myself that I owe a lot to Americans."

As for the respondents who do not use any of the labels "French," "American," or "French American," they tend to see themselves either above or below the national level, or both. A few feel that they are in a "no man's land" between the French and the American world.

> I regard myself as a citizen of the world more than anything else, since I constantly travel to different countries for my job as a travel consultant.

> I feel either global, or Breton [speaker's local origins], nothing in between. Frankly I don't care for flags and nations.

> I am not French any longer, but still not an American or even French American, because I have such a thick French accent in English.

The presence of a distinctive French accent in many first-generation French immigrants is a definite marker of ethnicity—an issue to which we shall return in Chapter 7.

Variability in Self-Identification

Self-labeling is only a preliminary cue to subjective identity, and may actually be deceptive: Labels have a semblance of permanency in people's minds, and as such, they fail to account for the fluid nature of

Table 6.2
Variability in Self-Identification (N = 96 respondents)

	%
Always feel more French	17.7
Always feel more American	12.5
Alternately feel more French or more American	43.0
Never feel more French or more American	24.0
Don't know	2.0

ethnicity. We must keep in mind that acculturation is an ongoing process, which means that ethnic identification is subject to variation not only from one individual to another, but also at the intra-individual level. In order to address this issue, I asked the respondents if there had been times or circumstances in their lives when they had felt more American or more French, and if so, to elaborate (Item # 12 in the Appendix).

Table 6.2 shows that 17.7 percent of the respondents report that they always feel more French, versus 12.5 percent who always feel more American. Almost half of them (43 percent) report that they alternate between feeling more French and feeling more American. The remaining 24 percent, besides the 2 percent who did not provide an answer, report that they never feel more French or more American, evidencing fusion of the two identities.

Those who always feel more French are sometimes rather assertive about it, regardless of citizenship status or length of residence in the United States (58 years in one case).

> I *never* feel more American than French, even after so many years [over half a century] here. *Everyone* sees me as French, and that's the way I *want* it to be.

> I am a dual citizen, but I've *always* felt more French because of my values, my love of art, my whole way of thinking, my relating to people.

> My English is so horrible that I always feel more French, even after 32 years in this country.

As in the case of self-labeling, some of the long-term U.S. residents indicate that they are conflicted about feeling more French than American, but they can be quick to offer rationalizations for it.

> I am ashamed to say so, because the United States has given me
> so much, but I *always* feel more French than American. For one
> thing, I like being a foreigner [speaker's own term, despite his U.S.
> citizenship and perfect command of English], it's an advantage, it
> makes you exotic, it gives you a more international outlook.

Those who feel more French all the time cover a whole range of marital statuses: One is unmarried, five are members of all-French couples, and eleven have non-French spouses. Conversely, those who feel more American all the time include not only nine individuals married to Americans, but also three who have French spouses. The expected tendency for members of all-French couples to feel more French all the time is negated in part by these last three cases, as well as the cases of six other inmarried individuals who alternate between feeling French and feeling American.

Among the few who always feel more American is a respondent who arrived in 1974, at a time when the pressure to assimilate as fast as possible had diminished in this country. He felt more American even before leaving France on a one-way ticket, determined as he was to become a "self-made man," which he has succeeded in doing. Ironically, he still has not acquired U.S. citizenship after 20 years of residence in this country. Others who also always feel more American invoke national politics, lifestyle, or language.

> Overall I feel more American because I participate in politics here.
> I felt especially strongly about being an American when my son was
> in Vietnam, fighting as a member of the U.S. army.

> As a young person, I realized that I respected the American lifestyle
> more than the French lifestyle, and I still feel that way.

> I feel more American *all* the time [while exclusively French in terms
> of citizenship] because I work with Americans and like the work
> lifestyle. It is more competitive than in France, but people are much
> more disciplined here.

> Basically I feel more American because of the language I speak all
> the time here.

The respondents who report alternating between feeling more French and feeling more American can be regarded as evidencing "coordinate" ethnic identification. Those who report never feeling either more French or more American can be regarded as evidencing "compound" ethnic identification. By borrowing the terms "coordinate" and "compound" from the field of bilingualism, I mean to highlight an interesting parallel: Just as first-generation immigrants may keep their native language and English on two different "tracks" in the thinking process, their two ethnic identification modes may never totally fuse into a single identity, remaining coordinate rather than becoming compound.

The 42 respondents in my sample who demonstrate coordinate identification exhibit recurring patterns, which are listed here in order of frequency of occurrence in the data.

- Feeling more French during the first few years in this country, more American later in life. "When I first came to the United States eighteen years ago, I spoke French with my husband and my French friends, I read French newspapers. Then gradually, as the years went by, I opened my mind to the American culture." Another respondent is quick to specify that he now feels more American than he did earlier, "except in two areas: food and political involvement."

- Feeling more French in the United States, but more American in France. One respondent sees this pattern as inevitable, due to self-fulfilling prophecy: "For the American people I am French, but for the French I am an American." The reverse pattern (feeling more French in France and more American in the United States) rarely occurs in my data.

- Feeling more American in terms of work, the workplace, and business in general.

- Feeling more French in the following aspects of everyday life: food patterns and table manners; cultural activities and the arts; matters of the heart, especially romance; beauty, fashion and clothes.

- Feeling more American in terms of hobbies, especially more adventurous outdoor activities.

- Feeling more American in political matters, especially when the United States is being criticized. Only a few respondents report feeling more French than American at the political level, despite their previously mentioned interest in newscasts from France.

- Feeling more French in the presence of other French people living in the United States, but more American in the presence of French people newly arrived or visiting from France.

Some salient features emerge from this inventory. In the minds of the respondents who demonstrate coordinate identification, the French world seems to be associated with home life (especially food patterns), cultural activities and the arts, matters of the heart, and personal aesthetics. The American world, on the other hand, seems to be associated with work and business, hobbies (especially sports), and political matters.

A few respondents give evidence of being particularly skilled at functioning as "cultural chameleons," avoiding internal conflict about their dual identity by turning the situation to their advantage and getting the best of both worlds through careful identity management.

> I have a way of totally adapting to the immediate environment. When I'm in the States I act and think as an American, and when I'm in France I switch on the French side of me, it's that simple!

> I feel more French most of the time in the States. But sometimes I *make* myself feel more American if I'm in circumstances in which I fit better that way.

> I really feel American when I attend a ceremony for U.S. war veterans. But when I was doing my time in the U.S. army, shortly after coming over here, they sent me to Germany, and you'd better believe that I quickly connected with some of the French military officers there, because they managed to eat much better than we did . . . I had some fantastic meals with them!

The general picture resulting from these findings is one of variable ethnicity at both the inter- and intra-individual levels. Fluctuations in the "national belonging" indexes evidence varying degrees of "Frenchness" and "Americanness" in different individuals, or in one and the same individual according to time and circumstances. However, only 12.5 percent of the respondents report always feeling more American, which clearly points to a certain degree of maintenance of French identity in a majority of cases—an interesting parallel to my analysis of self-labeling in the previous section.

MENTAL REPRESENTATIONS OF A DUAL WORLD

A number of queries in my interviews addressed the respondents' perceptions of their dual world. The large amount of data elicited through these (most often open-ended) questions will now be analyzed in two stages. We first briefly focus on French immigrants' perceptions of American attitudes toward the French world, in order to set up the general psychological context in which the maintenance of French identity occurs in the United States. We then turn to the respondents' own mental representations of their "old" and their "new" worlds, as directly stated by them.

Perceived Attitudes of Americans toward the French World

French immigrants are in a special position regarding their national heritage, given the high regard in which it is generally held in the United States. A well-known American observer of the international scene notes that "France remains in some ways the cultural capital of the world" (Hall 1990: 93). The influence it has had on American life and culture is, according to another American author, "almost beyond measure" (Kunz 1969: 83). France is also a country favored by visitors, and its history, language, and culture are the subject of many educational programs in this country. Consequently, Americans can be expected to have a certain degree of familiarity with the French world and some personal opinions about it.

Participants in my study were asked to report on their perceptions of such views on the part of Americans. They first had to assess how much they think Americans like each of the following: France as a country, French people, the French language, and the French culture (Item #67 in the Appendix). Each of these items was to be rated separately along a three-point scale ranging from "Very much" to "Not at all." Respondents were then asked to state how much prestige they think the French language and the French culture have in the United States (Item #68 in the Appendix). Another three-point scale ranging from "High" to "Low" was used for each of these two items.

When analyzing the data, I converted the three points of each scale

Table 6.3
Perceived American Attitudes toward the French World (Maximum score = 3)

	Average score
"Americans like France as a country"	2.6
"Americans like French people"	2.1
"Americans like the French language"	2.7
"Americans like the French culture"	2.7
Prestige of the French language in USA	2.5
Prestige of the French culture in USA	2.6

to numbers: 3 for Very much (in the first question) or High (in the second question); 2 for Somewhat or Medium; 1 for Not at all or Low. A rating of 1.5 would reflect an intermediate answer such as Medium to Low. The numbers thus obtained were added separately for each of the four items in Question #67 and two items in Question #68, then averaged for the set of respondents in each case.

Table 6.3 lists the average ratings for all six items in the order in which they appeared in the interview. As we can see, two of them have identical ratings of 2.7 (the maximum being 3), and all other ratings range between 2.6 and 2.1. It suggests that, generally speaking, the respondents attribute to Americans rather positive attitudes about the French world. However, the various average ratings reveal some interesting differences. The respondents are of the opinion that Americans like the French *language* and the French *culture* best (2.7, which is close to Very much), and France as a *country* almost as much (2.6). French *people*, on the other hand, only get a rating of 2.1, which is very close to Somewhat; a few respondents attributed their low ratings to the fact that Americans consider the French as generally "stuck up" and unkind to foreign visitors in France. Interestingly, these findings correspond, at a general level, to the judgment of a contemporary historian of the French in France.

> French people often feel that they are misunderstood by foreigners, that they are insufficiently appreciated, unloved. They are quite right. Foreigners undoubtedly love France as a place, as a beautiful country, but they do not on the whole like the French as a people. This is particularly true of the English-speaking world. The British

visit France more than they visit any other foreign country; over a
third of them have been to France; but only 2% say they admire the
French and very few indeed would like to live among them. . . . The
Americans, who do not have the handicap of having been traditional
enemies of France for centuries, generally feel they have little in
common with the country that once helped them in their War of
Independence. (Zeitlin 1983: 5)

As for the prestige of the French language and the French culture in
the United States, my respondents gave them respective ratings of 2.5
(half way between Medium and High) and 2.6 (slightly closer to High).
In most cases, the prestige ratings were exactly the same for language
and culture, but a few respondents gave a lower rating to the French
language, arguing that its prestige is declining, particularly on the
West Coast because of the growing importance of Spanish and various
Asian languages.

The generally positive perceived attitudes of Americans toward the
French world are likely to have an impact on French immigrants' own
images of their dual world. They can also be seen as an incentive to
maintain a certain degree of French identity in the United States.

Internalized Images of the French and the American World

Ethnic identity is based in part on a "we versus they" model of the
world in people's minds. The existence of such a model in a particular
immigrant population can be documented through a detailed examination of its members' internalized images of their two worlds.

The Two Countries and Their People

An easy entry into immigrants' mental representations of their "old"
world is to ask them what aspects of it they miss the most, if any. In
answer to this question (Item #62 in the Appendix), only three participants in my study claim that they do not miss any aspect of the French
world. At the other end of the continuum, one respondent asserts that
she misses "everything, even after 34 years of residence in the United
States." Other responses cover a wide range of items, the total amount
of tokens being 303, due to multiple answers by many of the 96 respondents. They cluster around seven major themes, which are listed

here in order of frequency of occurrence in the data; the components within each category are also rank ordered for frequency.

1. The country itself (70 tokens): Paris and/or specific regions (usually the respondent's place of origin) with their distinctive characteristics; the beauty of the countryside, its small villages, back roads, old structures including wells; particular types of public places such as cafés, small-scale restaurants, street markets, bakeries, and *pétanque* courses; also the "human size" of France and its proximity to other European countries.

2. Family and friends (57 tokens). This category is particularly salient in the case of respondents who emigrated less than ten years ago, as might have been expected. Some of those who have been here much longer make it clear that their responses would have been different in the past: "I don't miss anything of France now, but at first I really missed my family." It should also be noted that older individuals may no longer have any living relatives and friends in France, which obviously skews the data regarding the respondents' ties with their families of origin. The strength of such ties is evidenced by younger individuals' comments such as "The only thing I miss of France is my family," or "If I go back, it will only be because of my family and friends."

3. Cultural treasures and intellectual/artistic life (51 tokens): historical monuments, castles and museums in various parts of France; French literature, theater and films; intellectual life in general, knowledge of history, interest in the arts.

4. Food and wine (45 tokens). Faithful to the renown of French food products and cuisine, almost half of the respondents indicate that they miss them. One individual states that he misses "nothing other than the food in France, not even the family." The national preoccupation for food is evidenced by the detailed nature of some answers, with specification of the exact items missed. Among the most frequently mentioned are cheese, pork products (*charcuterie* or, in one respondent's almost tearful use of a familiar term, *cochonailles*), bread, pastry, fowl, and venison. Some particular types of cheese are mentioned, often corresponding to the respondents' respective regional origins (for instance, camembert for those from Normandie), which shows that food traditions of one's local area can have a persistent hold on people, even at a distance.

5. General quality of life (31 tokens): limited work time, long vacations, much unplanned leisure time.

6. Interpersonal relations beyond family and friends (30 tokens): strong social bonds with people in general; enjoyment of conversation, particularly at mealtimes; *joie de vivre*, wit, and laughter; teasing, even across gender lines; well-mannered children; respect for older people.

7. Ideology (9 tokens): solidarity, stability, humanism, respect for personal privacy on the part of the media, respect for tradition.

This inventory suggests that first-generation French immigrants miss a number of elements of the French world. What are, on the other hand, their preferred aspects of life in the United States? Responses to this interview question (Item #61 in the Appendix) reveal generally positive feelings toward the American world. Six respondents answer that they "like everything" here, and one prefaces his listing of specific items by remarking that he really loves this country. Only two individuals indirectly show negative feelings, one asserting that what she likes best here is "the lower cost of living, that's about it," and the other one expressing deeply-felt ambivalence: "I have my husband of many years here, and also my children and grandchildren, but that's all."

No other respondents made any mention of their spouses or offspring in this part of the interview, simply because they (correctly) assumed that such information did not correspond to the intent of the question. But it is obvious that their family ties in this country constitute a major factor of social integration.

A high proportion of the 96 respondents gave multiple responses in answer to my question about their favorite aspects of life in the United States. The total number of tokens is 226, with some of the same items mentioned by several respondents. They cluster around five major themes, which are listed here in order of frequency of occurrence; the component items are also rank ordered for frequency within each category.

1. Ideology (58 tokens): individual freedom; social mobility and absence of class barriers; valuation of hard work and success; encouragement of initiative and independence. The notion of freedom is the second most frequently occurring item in response to Question #61, with 29 tokens; respondents appreciate having the chance to "be a free spirit" or "act as a free agent with nobody or nothing to stop you." Social mobility and the perceived absence of class consciousness, also frequently mentioned, are often contrasted with the situation in France. One respondent who was "part of the proletariat in France" appreciates his professional position here; another one reports that some of her relatives visiting from France were shocked when they once saw her (a

baker) shaking hands with a highly positioned lawyer who patronized her store.

2. General quality of life (55 tokens): practical aspects of everyday life; child rearing practices; outdoor activities. The first item, with 39 tokens, is the most frequently occurring in responses to Question #61. Many respondents highly value the existence of conveniences and material comfort in their daily lives: easy shopping in stores due to a good selection of products, long business hours, and a service orientation; simplified chores at home thanks to mechanical help; spacious and comfortable houses. As for child-rearing practices, they are seen by several respondents as "better for human growth and development than French practices," particularly in comparison with "repressive methods in French schools."

3. Interpersonal relations (43 tokens): generally easy contact with people, openness and friendliness; informal ways such as the use of first names; generous hospitality; absence of frequent criticism "as compared to what happens in France."

4. Opportunities (35 tokens). A number of respondents refer to opportunities in general, which they see as "endless" or "unlimited." Others refer to specific opportunities: easy access to any kind of information; ability to get an education at any age, retrain for a different career, or move to a new job.

5. The country itself (35 tokens). Most of the responses falling into this category have to do with the diversity of people and cultures in the United States. Other aspects of the country at large mentioned by respondents are the beauty of natural sites such as national parks, as well as a general sense of spaciousness in cities and the countryside.

This inventory and the preceding one reveal rather different images of the French and the American world in the respondents' minds. Particularly striking is the fact that ideology, their most salient reason for liking the United States, is the aspect of France they miss the least. Almost as important in their visualization of America is what they regard as a good quality of life; on the other hand, the country itself is not salient in their mental representations. This is in contrast with their visualization of the French world: If we put aside the purely personal side of it (family and friends), the most salient components are France itself, its cultural treasures and intellectual/artistic life and its food and wine.

These findings closely parallel the previously discussed answers to another interview question (Item #60 in the Appendix) concerning aspects of life in France that the respondents may have been glad to leave behind when they emigrated. Six of the ten categories of features repertoried in Chapter 3 are an almost exact counterpart to the respondents' preferred aspects of life in the United States. The following were perceived (by some) as negative features of France: lack of personal freedom, the organizational structure, the political situation, the economic situation, social stratification, and practical aspects of life such as shopping habits.

Additional validation is provided by answers to two other interview questions (Items #75 and 76 in the Appendix) that actually produced responses similar to the previous ones. Respondents were asked to go beyond their personal likes and dislikes and "free associate" about their global images of the French and the American world. Despite the instructions, most of their responses duplicate to a very large extent the material already covered and, therefore, will not be discussed here.

The French Language and American English

Our examination of French immigrants' mental representations of their dual world would not be complete without a consideration of language, a component of ethnicity often hailed as central to it (see for example Fishman 1984, Gudykunst 1988, Heller 1987).

The following discussion is based on interview data obtained through free association methods that aimed at eliciting, from the 96 individuals included in my final sample, spontaneous reactions about the French language and American English. Respondents were first asked to mention, separately for each of the two languages, ten adjectives they associate with it (Items #73 and #74 in the Appendix). The order of these questions was often reversed in order to avoid any potential bias, and respondents were instructed to stop listing adjectives as soon as the flow "dried up," since the actual number of tokens was less important than the spontaneous nature of the data.

Most responses contain fewer than ten tokens for each of the two languages. Their total number amounts to 790, which represents an average of 8.2 adjectives per respondent for the two languages. There are 433 tokens for French, an average of 4.5 per respondent, and 357 tokens for American English, an average of 3.7 per respondent.

The separate analysis of the data for each language proceeded as follows. First, I tallied all the adjectives associated by the respondents with the language in question and rank ordered them in terms of frequency of occurrence. Those with the highest frequencies were then selected to serve as starting points in the construction of clusters of conceptually related items. Other adjectives found their place in these initial clusters or occasionally formed clusters of their own. Finally, when an adjective only had one to three tokens and did not fit in any of the existing clusters, it was regarded as insufficiently representative and eliminated from further consideration. The final lists obtained by this method consist of 364 adjectives regrouped into 15 clusters of conceptually related items in the case of French, and 303 adjectives regrouped into 14 clusters of conceptually related items in the case of English. These clusters will now be enumerated in order of frequency of occurrence, as measured by the total number of tokens of the adjectives included in them.

Two clusters of conceptually related adjectives stand out in the case of the French language: The respondents regard it as beautiful-attractive (67 tokens) and musical-poetic (52 tokens). It is also seen as precise-clear-logical (40 tokens), refined-elegant-courteous (36 tokens), expressive-colorful (34 tokens), rich-complex (27 tokens), romantic-passionate (25 tokens), subtle-nuanced (16 tokens), traditional-ancient (10 tokens), diplomatic (8 tokens), literary (8 tokens), gentle (5 tokens), humorous-funny (5 tokens). On the negative side, French is regarded by some respondents as difficult (28 tokens) and by a few as pompous-snobbish (5 tokens).

In the case of American English, the two most frequently occurring clusters of conceptually related adjectives show the respondents to regard it as primarily direct-precise-clear (60 tokens) and practical-technical-efficient (55 tokens). It is also considered as rich-diverse-flexible (34 tokens), easy-comfortable (30 tokens), international-universal (18 tokens), musical-poetic (14 tokens), fast-vibrant (14 tokens), expressive-colorful (10 tokens), modern-future oriented (6 tokens), beautiful-nice (5 tokens), and popular (5 tokens). There are only a few negative features to counterbalance this positive image of American English. Some respondents perceive it as difficult-irregular (26 tokens), in contradiction with the previously mentioned respondents who perceive it as easy-comfortable. It is also regarded by some as harsh-sloppy (20 tokens) and by a few as dominant-controlling (6 tokens).

These two inventories indicate that the respondents have mostly positive images of both languages: The proportion of positive adjectives is 91 percent in the case of the French language and 82.8 percent in the case of American English. However, the two most salient features attributed to each language differ greatly in nature. They are in the realm of aesthetics for the French language and pragmatics for American English—a contrast that strongly parallels other images in the respondents' minds.

Their perception of American English as primarily direct-precise-clear and practical-technical-efficient corresponds to the saliency, in their mental representations of the American world, of work and business, an ideology of individual enterprise, and a good quality of life especially in terms of practical aspects of everyday life. As for their perception of the French language as primarily beautiful-attractive and musical-poetic, it could easily be dismissed as nonsignificant, since French immigrants are obviously not unique in attributing such hyperbolic qualities to their language of origin. However, we will see that additional data reinforce the parallel we see emerging here between, on the one hand, the respondents' perception of their native language and, on the other hand, the emphasis on cultural treasures and intellectual/artistic life in their images of the French world.

Respondents were asked to perform another free association task that consisted in completing the sentence "To me the French language is like . . ." (Item #77 in the Appendix). Their responses fall into five major thematic categories. They are listed here in order of frequency of occurrence, as measured by the number of tokens in each of them.

- Music and poetry (35 tokens). Examples: "To me the French language is like a song," "poetry," or "music to my ears."

- Home, family, and friendship (19 tokens). Examples: "To me the French language is like an old friend," "the only way I can relate to my babies or my pets," or "the result of my childhood and formative years."

- Sensory experience (15 tokens): vision, smell, taste and touch, occasionally overlapping and resulting in synesthesia. Examples: "To me the French language is like bubbling champagne," or "a field of lavender in bloom with a lovely smell."

- Water in motion (7 tokens). Examples: "To me the French language is like a fountain," "a wave in the ocean," or "a flowing river."

- Romance and love (6 tokens). Examples: "To me the French language is like falling in love," or "a sound of love."

In addition to these 82 tokens, there were a few responses that did not fit in any of these major themes. For instance, two of them evoke the liveliness of the French language: "To me the French language is like a runner or jogger," or "something alive." Only one response indicated a negative perception of French as being too conservative: "To me the French language is like a dinosaur."

Some respondents could not refrain from elaborating on their brief answers to the sentence completion test, volunteering strongly worded comments:

> The French language is my real self, everything that's close to me.

> For me the French language has a very sentimental value. If I were to lose it, I would be cutting off part of what I am, ninety percent of it. It would be like a lobotomy.

How does this obviously strong attachment to their language of origin influence French immigrants' perception of its social significance at various levels? Participants in my study were asked to comment on the place of the French language in French culture and society (Item #78 in the Appendix). I often prolonged the discussion, asking respondents to comment also on the current influence of English on the French language in France, particularly in relation to the development of the European Union.

The respondents' answers are often rather assertive: The French language is regarded as central to life in France, "the backbone of its culture and society," or "the core of France, partly for historical reasons." A few lament the present state of the language, pointing to a lowering of standards and the spreading of "bad French" (slang, careless speech, poor writing and spelling) particularly among young people.

> My grandmother used to say that having bad spelling was like wearing a dirty shirt. . . . But now people don't care that much, you can even get hired for a job if you can't spell properly.

Many more respondents regard the inroads of English as the major threat to their native language, which is somewhat ironic, since they have adopted English as an everyday language and cannot help being influenced by it in their own speech (Lindenfeld 1997). Some wish that French people would "stop using American words or 'Frenchizing' them." A few want tighter control over language by members of the

French Academy and other purists. Most respondents, however, realize that language cannot be governed in such manner and that the spread of English is inevitable. They occasionally express the hope that its influence will be limited to certain areas, such as the business world, and that the French language will remain alive in other aspects of life in France, especially in the world of literature and the arts.

As for the competition between the two languages within the European Union, respondents are divided in their opinions about its resolution. A few consider that the battle has already been lost. But many others think that, while French is undeniably losing ground at the European level, it will definitely survive at the national level.

> French will *never* disappear in France, because the French will *never* let it die. They take language very seriously, they are proud and protective of their language, and they *should* be!

In order to further explore the respondents' mental representations of their dual world, I asked them (Item #79 in the Appendix) to create scenarios in which the French language and American English, or France and the United States, would be represented as protagonists in an encounter. While a number of respondents declined the invitation to perform this admittedly difficult task, 77 of them provided rich material that, in many cases, is highly revealing of their perceptions of the relationship between the two components of their dual world.

The daunting diversity of their scenarios first defied analysis, but it soon became apparent that the notion of conflict could be used as an organizing principle to interpret them. Almost half (37 out of 77) of the "scripts" provided by the respondents reveal no conflict about the relationship between the French and the American world: accounts of the imagined encounter are either positive (21) or neutral (16). The remaining 40 responses, however, reveal varying degrees of conflict.

The 21 positive scripts picture the protagonists as getting along, or trying to do so, on the basis of complementarity or (much less frequently) commonality of features. The imagined interaction may include playful fighting or harmless teasing between the two protagonists; it always ends on a conciliatory note.

> I see American English as a fast sports car with horsepower, and the French language as an elegant car but not a workhorse. They complement each other beautifully.

There is an animated French musketeer demonstrating his prowess with a sword, and a more phlegmatic American cowboy using a lasso. They try to accommodate each other. They end up shaking hands.

It's like a Siamese cat and a French poodle. They pick on each other, but they get along fine.

The 16 neutral scripts represent the two protagonists as different from each other, but co-existing peacefully because neither of them is superior/dominant or inclined to confrontation.

I would represent the French language as a river and American English as a waterfall. Each has its own merits.

There are two ice-skaters. The one representing France is dancing on ice; the one representing the United States is doing speed and distance skating. They are equal, neither is better than the other one, and they don't interfere with each other.

The character representing the United States is business-like, earnest, outgoing, has a go-for-it attitude. The character representing France is enjoying life. They don't have much in common, their goals are different, so they can barely talk to each other.

As for the 40 negative scripts, they are most often based on perceived dominance patterns on one side or the other. Interestingly, respondents who perceive the interaction in this way are almost equally divided into those who attribute superiority and/or dominance to the French world and those who attribute it to the American world. In several cases, descriptions of the imagined encounter include scenes of actual fighting. Other scripts, while they are not as "warlike," stress the impossibility of mutual understanding between the two protagonists, because of their sharp differences.

I would have France as a rooster and the United States as a lion. Each of them is chauvinistic, so they have a real fight.

My picture of France is de Gaulle giving a nationalistic speech in Canada, with a bottle of wine and flowers next to him. My picture of the United States is the Statue of Liberty, which will clobber de Gaulle.

Table 6.4
Preferences Regarding Country of Residence in Relation to Years in USA (N = number of respondents)

	USA %	France %	Both %	Other/no pref %
Under 10 yrs (N = 11)	36.3	27.3	9.1	27.3
10-25 yrs (N = 31)	64.5	12.9	9.7	12.9
Over 25 yrs (N = 54)	55.6	1.8	27.8	14.8
Total (N = 96)	56.2	8.3	19.8	15.6

> It's an encounter between a bull representing the French language,
> and a bullfighter representing American English. The bull is stable
> and obstinate, the bullfighter is constantly changing course. In the
> end the bull is the stronger one and wins.

It may not be too much of a leap of imagination to regard these scenarios as metaphorical representations of the experience of first-generation French immigrants, as they attempt to strike a balance between their French and their American worlds. Which way would the scale tip, if this delicate equilibrium were put to the test?

THE "REALITY TEST"

In order to test the degree of attachment of French immigrants to their country of origin, I devised an interview question (Item #59 in the Appendix) that required respondents to make a hypothetical choice between the United States and France as a country of permanent residence. It was worded as follows: "If you had a choice, in what country would you prefer to live just now?"

As indicated in Table 6.4, a majority of the respondents (56.2 percent) are quite content to live in the United States. A total of 28.1 percent would prefer to live either in France (8.3 percent) or in both countries (19.8 percent). The remaining 15.6 percent have no preference or would prefer some country other than France and the United States.

An interesting relationship exists between the respondents' preference patterns and the number of years they have spent in this country (see Table 6.4). Among those who have under 10 years of U.S. residence, the rate of preference for living here (36.3 percent) is more or less equal to the combined rate (36.4 percent) of preference for France or for both countries. However, in the two sets of respondents who have respectively 10–25 years and over 25 years of U.S. residence, the rates of preference for living here (64.5 and 55.6 percent respectively) are much higher than the combined rates (22.6 and 29.6 percent respectively) of preference for France or for both countries. These last two sets of respondents show an interesting contrast in their rates of preference for France (12.9 and 1.8 percent respectively) or for both countries (9.7 and 27.8 percent respectively).

The common threads in these various patterns are work and family. The rate of preference for living in the United States is highest (64.5 percent) in the set of respondents with 10 to 25 years of U.S. residence, who all have family and/or work obligations here at the present time. As for the respondents who have over 25 years of U.S. residence, they often want to remain close to their families in this country, even if they are now free of work obligations.

The 19 respondents who would like to live in both countries (usually half the time in each) are mostly long-term U.S. residents whose children are grown and who are either retired or approaching retirement. Their vision (or experience) of a life shared between their country of origin and their adopted country would be an impossible dream for many younger people because of work and family obligations. It should be noted that all respondents who would prefer to live only in France, regardless of length of U.S. residence, are in this country because of marriage with an American and/or work.

A number of comments show some individuals to be realistic about their expressed preferences. The first two have been here under 10 years, the third has 18 years of U.S. residence, and the fourth 47 years.

> I prefer living in the States because of the job opportunities.

> France is my preference of course, and I hope that my [American] husband and I can go back after our daughter's education.

> I would like to live in France, but work in the United States.

> My preference would be half the time in each of the two countries because my friends and the rest of my family are in France, but my [American] husband and children and grandchildren are in the States.

It is one thing to dream about one's preference regarding country of residence, it is another thing to face the reality of potential re-

Table 6.5
Patterns of Hypothetical Re-Adaptation to France in Relation to Years in USA (N = 96 respondents)

	Very easy %	Rather easy %	Not easy %	Other %
Under 10 yrs (N = 11)	27.2	36.4	36.4	0.0
10-25 yrs (N = 31)	16.1	22.6	54.8	6.5
Over 25 yrs (N = 54)	20.4	24.0	53.7	1.9
Total (N = 96)	19.8	25.0	52.1	3.1

adaptation problems in the hypothetical case of permanent return to one's native country. A question in my interview (Item #64 in the Appendix) addressed this issue. Respondents were asked to assess whether they would re-adapt to France very easily, rather easily, or not easily, if they were to go back there permanently.

As shown in Table 6.5, only 19.8 percent of the respondents think that they would re-adapt to France very easily and 25 percent rather easily, while 52.1 percent indicate that they would not re-adapt easily. The first two figures amount to a total of 44.8 percent of "positive" answers, versus approximately 52 percent "negative" answers, suggesting that many respondents are aware of the fact that affective ties with one's homeland are not sufficient to ensure easy re-adaptation. The remaining 3.1 percent had evasive answers such as "I really don't know."

In Table 6.5, the respondents have been divided again into three sets according to length of residence in the United States. Even among those who have been here under ten years, 36.4 percent indicate that they would not easily re-adapt to France. The rate increases to 54.8 percent among those with 10 to 25 years of U.S. residence, and 53.7 percent among those who have been here more than 25 years.

It may come as a surprise that this last set has a proportion of 20.4 percent of respondents thinking that they would re-adapt very easily to France, as compared to 16.1 percent among those with 10 to 25 years of U.S. residence. The obvious explanation lies again in the difference between retired or soon-to-be-retired people, and those who still hold jobs, as illustrated by the following remarks, the first one by a 42-year-old working woman, the second by a retired man in his late sixties.

> I would re-adapt to France very easily, except if I could not find a job.

It would be very easy, I would live in a small village in the Pyrénées [the kind of place the speaker left long ago for economic reasons].

Whatever their age group and length of residence in the United States, most respondents have one thing in common: a strong desire to have their children feel "at home" in this country, which is both a factor and an indicator of their own social integration. An interview question addressed the issue in those terms: "Do you want your children to feel well integrated in American society?" (Item #65 in the Appendix). The four possible answers ranged from "Yes, very much" to "Not at all." An overwhelming majority of the 77 respondents who have children answered either "Yes, very much" (29) or "Yes" (40). Only 4 answered "Not really" and 1 "Not at all"; the remaining 3 did not know.

In the light of these responses, it should not come as a surprise that only one of the respondents, in answer to another interview question (Item #58 in the Appendix), reported frequent attendance of her children at French cultural events in the United States. All others divided almost equally between those who reported occasional attendance and those who could not even think of one occasion when their offspring had taken part in such activities.

The interview also included a query (Item #66 in the Appendix) about the parents' preferences regarding marriage partners for their offspring. While French partners were favored by 14 respondents and American partners by 4, an overwhelming majority (59 out of the 77 respondents who have children) stated that they have no preference. Many remarked that the choice has to be left up to their children, which serves as a reminder of the significance of individual decision making in the lives of modern-day French people.

The maintenance of a French identity in the second generation is clearly overshadowed by integration into American society, as acknowledged by the respondents. In answer to a question concerning their children's self-identification (Item #45 in the Appendix), only two French parents report cases of children (one in each family) who feel more French than American. Other respondents divide into approximately two-thirds reporting that their children (including a few who grew up in France) feel more American than French, and one-third whose children feel that they are a blend of the two.

Within this general context of integration into American society, one remaining mechanism for the maintenance of a French identity centers around the retention and transmission of the French language. We saw

earlier that first-generation French immigrants' mental representations of the French world include many positive images of their
language of origin. We now need to examine some behavioral manifestations of these perceptions, with particular focus on language skills
and use in later generations.

7

The French Linguistic Heritage

The crucial role of language in ethnicity has been amply demonstrated not only in the work of language science researchers, but also in the reality of people's lives. We can readily think of instances of language conflicts that have pitted groups of speakers against one another in various parts of the world. A case in point is the current situation in Québec, a province of Canada in which French speakers' organized opposition to the English language has had serious political repercussions.

In the United States, French remains an important language in terms of numbers of speakers. According to the 1990 census, it is spoken at home by 1,930,404 persons five years and over, which places it in third rank in the nation—immediately after Spanish, declared as the language spoken at home by 17,345,064 persons five years and over. An overwhelming majority of the speakers of French living in the United States have their origins in America, particularly in Canada. The centrality of language in the settlement history of French-speaking Canadian immigrants is well documented.

> French heritage (more specifically, French Canadian in New England and Cajun in Louisiana) was perceived to be integrally tied

to language maintenance and the maintenance of the Catholic religion (the latter more true in New England than in Louisiana).
(Barrish 1992: 42)

However, there have been signs of erosion of the French language in
the United States in recent years. Despite their long-standing network
of Catholic parishes and parochial schools, some French-speaking communities in New England have undergone rapid transformation in the
last few decades due to modernization and the lure of economic success
in mainstream American society (Parker 1983, Veltman 1987). The position of the French language is also precarious in Louisiana, although
efforts have been made in the last three decades to reinforce it through
concerted language planning (Blyth 1997, Valdman 1997, Waddell
1993). The current popularity of Cajun music and food should not make
us lose sight of the larger picture.

Hopeful language activists point out that Cajun culture is once
again being celebrated with vigorous pride, thanks to the cultural
revival that began in the mid-1960s and continues today. Yet the
social factors that originally contributed to language shift continue
today as well—modernization, industrialization, and migration.
(Blyth 1997:42)

In the Pacific region, the number of French speakers is relatively low
in most places. In California, a total of 132,657 persons five years and
over (0.44 percent of the total state population) declared French as a
home language in the 1990 census. The figure was 40,921 for Los Angeles County, one of five counties in the nation with the largest concentration of French ancestry groups; and 20,135 for the city of Los
Angeles. While these absolute numbers are not negligible, we must
keep in mind that they only represent a drop in an ocean of ethnic
diversity in southern California. A similar situation prevails in San
Francisco County: in 1990, there were 8,487 persons five years and over
declaring French as a home language.

In Oregon, the 1990 census figure was 10,854, representing 0.38 percent of the total state population. Numbers were particularly low in
semirural areas such as the Rogue Valley in southern Oregon. Jackson
County, for instance, had 765 persons five years and over declaring
French as a home language, 237 of whom live in Medford, the largest
town in the county. Some first-generation immigrants from France who

live in smaller towns or more isolated places in the area are obviously confronted with an essentially non-French speaking environment.

Given this situation, compounded by the lack of frequent contact in the United States between French-born individuals and speakers of French with Canadian or Caribbean origins, maintenance of the French linguistic heritage is a difficult task for direct immigrants from France—as attested by my data.

The analysis to be presented in this chapter is based on the 96 semi-formal interviews included in my final sample. We first focus on native language retention in the immigrant generation, then on transmission of the French linguistic heritage in subsequent generations. The chapter ends with some reflections on the role of the French language as a marker of ethnicity among French immigrants in the United States.

LANGUAGE RETENTION IN THE IMMIGRANT GENERATION

Most contemporary immigrants from France already have some knowledge of the English language when they arrive in the United States; for the few who do not, linguistic acculturation is an essential part of the adaptation process, since access to other speakers of French is limited. As a result, first-generation French immigrants who have lived here for a number of years are most often bilingual, with varying degrees of proficiency in English. Their bilingualism tends to be additive rather than subtractive: They rarely forget French, even if they speak English most of the time. In all my years of participant observation in California and Oregon, I have hardly ever come across cases of French-born individuals who could no longer speak French. One exception is a man in Los Angeles whose name had been given to me for potential participation in my study. After three decades of residence in the United States and no contacts with other natives of France, he could barely manage in the French language. I offered to interview him in English, but he declined because he was "ashamed" (his own term) of having lost touch with his language and culture of origin.

The actual participants in my study can all be considered as French-English bilinguals. However, their level of ability varies from one language to the other, as attested by their self-reports as well as my own observation of their speech.

Language Skills and Preferences

All 96 participants included in the final sample are native speakers of French. For most of them, it was the only language learned in infancy and childhood. One respondent who first learned Breton and three who first learned Basque, due to their regional origins, started learning French at age three or four and soon became dominant in that language. Nine other respondents were raised bilingually due either to mixed parentage or to place of residence (e.g., Alsace, which still has speakers of Alsatian, a Germanic language); but for all of them, French was the primary language throughout childhood and adolescence.

Where do these 96 native speakers of French now stand in terms of language dominance? In response to Question #21 in the interview, about half of them report that French is still their dominant language, regardless of length of residence in the United States (over 45 years in several cases). Only one-third of them consider English as their dominant language; the few remaining ones feel equally at ease in the two languages.

Detailed measurements of the respondents' language skills confirm that, generally speaking, they have a higher level of proficiency in French than they do in English. The primary method for obtaining such measurements was self-reporting. Two questions in the interview (Items #22 and 23 in the Appendix) were formulated in such a way as to facilitate the respondents' task of separately assessing their proficiency in the two languages. For each of the four basic skills (understanding, speaking, reading and writing) the individual had to choose a grade of Excellent, Good, Fair or Poor, or some intermediate grade.

The respondents' self-assessment of language skills corresponded closely to my own evaluations whenever I was able to make such comparisons. As mentioned earlier (Chapter 2), the semiformal interviews were often preceded and/or followed by informal conversations with the participants, which enabled me to assess their understanding and speaking skills in French, the language used almost exclusively in those circumstances. Only a few respondents gave me the chance to evaluate their reading and writing skills in French, but a certain level of proficiency was ensured in advance because of their schooling.

As for their English language skills, I had ample opportunities to assess two of them, namely understanding and speaking. The semiformal interviews were most often conducted face-to-face, and questions were usually asked in English. Although the respondents could choose

Table 7.1
Language Skills in the Immigrant Generation

	Average overall proficiency score *	Inter-individual range
French	15.5	16 - 11
English	13.7	16 - 7

*Perfect score =16

to answer in French, there was always sufficient material in English for an evaluation of speaking skills in that language. I also made it a practice to bring along an extra copy of the interview guide and occasionally ask respondents to read a question for themselves, which gave me a chance to assess their reading skills in English. Writing is the only English language skill for which I had to rely almost entirely on self-reporting.

When analyzing the data, I converted the grades of Poor, Fair, Good, and Excellent to numbers from 1 to 4, and intermediate grades accordingly. A respondent who is excellent in all four skills has an overall proficiency score of 16, one who is poor in all four skills has a score of 4, etc. These measurements lead to a general picture of proficiency in each of the two languages for my sample of participants at large.

As indicated in Table 7.1, some differences emerge between the respondents' language skills in French and in English. First of all, their average overall proficiency score for all four skills is 15.5 in French (only a half point off the "perfect" score), versus 13.7 in English. Second, the range of variation is narrower in French than it is in English: In the first case, individual scores range from 16 to 11, with an overwhelming majority of the respondents scoring 16; in the second case, they range from 16 to 7, with fewer than half of the respondents scoring 16. Finally, over half of the respondents (54 out of 96) have higher scores in French than they do in English, while 27 have equal scores in the two languages, and only 15 have higher scores in English. The slight discrepancy between the last two figures and the dominance patterns reported by the respondents (as discussed at the beginning of this section) must be attributed in part to the common persistence of a French accent in English, which "lowers the grade" for speaking skills even in the case of individuals who may be fluent in the language.

The rate of native language retention represented by these findings is rather impressive, given the respondents' average length of residence in the United States (27.2 years) and the fact that some of them have few or no opportunities to speak French. In answer to a question (Item #24 in the Appendix) about their current language use, an overwhelming majority of the respondents reports speaking either English most of the time and French sometimes (46 cases), or exclusively English (15 cases). Others report speaking either English and French equally (5 cases); or English, French, and a third language equally (3 cases). Fewer than one-third of the respondents report speaking French either most of the time (16 cases), or exclusively (11 cases).

On several occasions during my fieldwork, I was impressed with the level of French language skills in natives of France who had lived as isolated French speakers for many years in the United States. Such was the case of Mathilde, the 92-year-old woman who had emigrated as an 18-year-old WWI bride in 1920, at a time when nativist attitudes prevailed in this country and immigrants were expected to "forget" their languages of origin. Each of her two successive late husbands had instructed her to speak only English, so she had not used French regularly during her long life in this country. When I first contacted her on the phone, she still sounded like a native speaker and only had occasional difficulties remembering lexical items. In recent years, her retention of the language had been facilitated by regular contacts with a French-speaking family at the local Catholic church.

An important dimension of language retention for speakers of languages other than English is indeed the amount of contact they have with other native speakers. When asked how often they speak French with French-speaking friends in this country (Item #16 in the Appendix), 79 of the 96 respondents report that they always do so, and 15 that they sometimes do so. Among the 58 respondents who have French business acquaintances (see Chapter 5), 50 report that they always speak French with them and 8 that they sometimes do so.

Parallel to these findings regarding language use are the respondents' language preferences, which are indicated in their answers to Question #25 in the interview. As shown in Table 7.2, almost two-thirds of them (63.5 percent) prefer to speak French at home whenever possible; 16.7 percent prefer English as a home language, 13.5 percent have no preference, and 6.3 percent are undecided. The pattern is only slightly different for language preference in public: 55.2 percent prefer speaking French, 27.0 percent prefer English, 11.5 percent have no preference, and 6.3 percent are undecided; those who prefer speaking English in public often invoke rules of politeness.

Table 7.2
Language Preferences in the Immigrant Generation

	At home %	In public %
French	63.5	55.2
English	16.7	27.0
No preference	13.5	11.5
Undecided	6.3	6.3

This examination of language skills and preferences in a representative sample of first-generation French immigrants reveals a good deal of attachment to the French linguistic heritage. The analysis of other aspects of language retention, such as naming practices, confirms this general picture.

Naming Practices

French people who live in the United States tend to be strongly attached to their original names and resist pressures to alter them. My long-term observations regarding this issue concur with the empirical evidence provided by participants in my study. After years of residence in this country, most of the 96 respondents have not changed their first names to make them sound more American. Only 16 of them have done so, and the modifications have most often been minor, as we shall see. The first names appearing in the examples, followed by an indication of gender in parentheses, are the respondents' real names, in contrast with the fictitious first names that had to be used earlier (Chapter 3) in the description of individual trajectories.

The modification patterns emerging from the data are the following, in decreasing order of frequency:

- adoption of an American first name similar or equivalent to the French name (6 cases), e.g., Frank for François (m), Jim for Gilles (m). In the second case, upon being accidentally addressed as Jim, the respondent decided to adopt that name, rather than continue to suffer occasional gender confusion due to the mispronounciation of his French name as Jill.
- reduction of a compound first name to the first or second member of the pair (5 cases), e.g., Jean-Baptiste (m) to Jean pronounced

as /žã/; Marie-Thérèse (f) to Thérèse. The first respondent insists on the French pronunciation of his shortened name, so as to avoid potential gender confusion based on its spelling. The second respondent adamantly refuses to be called Theresa, "or, even worse, Terry," considering that she has made a sufficient compromise by reducing her given double name to a single one.

- adoption of an American nickname corresponding to the French first name (3 cases), e.g., Christine (f) or Christiane (f) to Chris. These shortened names are not necessarily used in co-ethnic situations.

- substitution of a middle name for a first name that was judged to be more difficult to pronounce (2 cases), e.g., Renée, Yvonne (f) to Yvonne.

- substitution of the equivalent French name for a Basque name that was less familiar to Americans.

The remaining 79 respondents in my sample have not changed their first names, despite a variety of problems:

- pronunciation difficulties, e.g., Annick (f) mispronounced with stress on the first syllable, and Jean-Michel (m) occasionally reduced to the first two syllables or replaced by Jamie.

- a combination of pronunciation and spelling problems, e.g., Chantal (f) mispronounced and misspelled as Chantel (and occasionally replaced by Candle or Chanterelle).

- potential gender equivocation, for example Jean-Marie (m) perceived as a female first name;

- misleading similarity with an American first name, e.g., Eliane (f) often changed to Ellen.

First-generation French immigrants are sometimes vociferous about attempts by Americans to "rename" them, especially when nicknames are used without their consent—a definite cultural *faux pas* by French standards.

> My first name is so difficult to pronounce that people have called me Gretchen, as if I were a woman, or Frenchy. But I still haven't changed it.

I would *never* change my first name, no way! I don't even let people
call me Dan.

As for last names, none of the 96 respondents has changed theirs,
despite frequent pronunciation problems and "suggested" modifications. A male respondent who happens to work in a wine shop is occasionally addressed as Mr. Chardonnay, a very rough approximation of
his French last name, which he still has no intention to change. Some
female respondents show a great deal of determination concerning the
preservation of their French maiden names, using them instead of, or
in addition to, their husbands' names—a pattern that is not unusual
in France, since women must use their maiden names throughout their
lives for a number of official and legal purposes.

> When I married my American husband, I made a point to keep my
> French maiden name and I still use it exclusively, although many
> Americans find it very difficult to pronounce.

> I got married in the United States, and at first I used only my
> husband's name. Then a few years ago I decided to start using my
> French maiden name in front of my married name. So now I've got
> this awfully long last name. . . . I *had* to do it, in reaction to my in-
> laws' influence. Just as I *had* to give typically French names [both
> of them compound names, with Marie as the first member] to our
> daughters. It was a battle between my husband and myself, but the
> in-laws had to stay out of it.

The selection of given names for their offspring is also illustrative of
first-generation immigrants' efforts to retain their French heritage.
Name giving, far from being a random act, often has a high degree of
symbolic significance even in Western industrialized societies, as
pointed out in a study of American women married to French men in
France.

> In the context of our international families, first names are a snap-
> shot of the parents' specific intent when the baby was born. If a
> typically American or French name was chosen, it is one of the first
> indelible cultural stamps in a series, with the mother tongue(s)
> coming a very close second. (Varro 1988: 145)

Let us examine, in the light of these remarks, the name distribution
of my respondents' children, on the basis of answers to Question #26

in the interview. Among the 89 married or formerly married French-born individuals in my sample, 58 have children who were born in the United States; other children born to them in France or some other country will not be considered here, since their names were not chosen in an American context. The 118 U.S.-born children divide as follows: 19 are the offspring of mononational (French + French) couples, 91 are the offspring of mixed couples whose non-French member is an American, and 8 are the offspring of mixed couples whose non-French member is a national other than French or American. We will not consider the last set in the analysis to follow, in order to avoid introducing a new variable, namely the presence of a parental language other than French or English in the household.

The names of the 110 children under consideration have been classified as typically American, typically French, or bilingual—the last category containing names that allow the child to "pass," rather than being clearly marked as American or French. A criterion for the classification of a name in one of the first two categories is its spelling, which is often linked to its pronunciation; for instance, Philip (with stressed first syllable) is considered as American, whereas Philippe (with stressed second syllable) as French. A number of my respondents made specific remarks about some of their children's names, underlining the significance of their choices.

> My son's name is *Damien* [pronounced the French way] spelled with an *e* after the *i*, it's not *Damian* [pronounced the American way].

> I have a daughter by the name of *Valerie* [pronounced the American way]; it's not *Valérie* [pronounced the French way] with an accent on the *e*.

Table 7.3 indicates that the first names of the immigrant generation's U.S.-born children fall almost equally into the three categories: 32.7 percent are typically French, 35.5 percent are bilingual, and 31.8 percent are typically American. But the proportions differ in families headed by two French parents and those headed by a mixed couple (French + American). In the first case, only 1 of the 19 children (5.2 percent) has what was at the time a typically American name, Sandra; others divide equally between typically French names (47.4 percent) and bilingual names (47.4 percent). Some of the French names, such as Françoise, are particularly indicative of a sense of nationalism, while

Table 7.3

First Names of the Immigrant Generation's U.S.-Born Children

	French names %	Bilingual Names %	American names %
Children of mononational couples (N = 19)	47.4	47.4	5.2
Children of mixed couples (N = 91)	29.7	33.0	37.3
Both types of children (N = 110)	32.7	35.5	31.8

at the same time lending themselves to potential Americanization in the future (Frances or Fran).

As for the names of the 91 children of mixed couples, they fall into the following categories: 29.7 percent are typically French, 33 percent are bilingual, and 37.3 percent are typically American. The proportion of French names is therefore significantly lower than the one we found in the mononational set (29.7 versus 47.4 percent). However, some of these French names are either compounds such as Marie-Pascale (f), or names that present potential pronunciation problems in English such as Etienne (m), attesting to the fact that attachment to the French heritage may override other considerations. Conversely, most of the American names appear to have been chosen with French speakers in mind: They are either strikingly similar to French names, for example, Alan (Alain in French), or easy to pronounce in French, for example, Tana (f).

The total inventory of 39 bilingual names for the children of both mononational and mixed (French + American) couples contains essentially two kinds of names with different frequencies: mostly "passing" names that are well known to both French and American people, such as Eric (9 cases) or Caroline (3 cases), and a few uncommon names such as Paul-Richard (1 case).

All in all, most participants in this study show a strong degree of attachment to French tradition in their naming practices. Few of them have changed their own names; as for the children's given names, they are for the most part typically French or bilingual, and few of the typically American names are either totally different from French names or difficult to pronounce in French. These practices seem indicative of the respondents' intent regarding the preservation of the French heritage. Does the reality correspond to their intent? An examination of their transmission of the French language to their offspring will provide us with some answers to this question.

LANGUAGE TRANSMISSION IN LATER GENERATIONS

French immigrants in the United States are in a special position regarding language transmission: unlike speakers of little-known languages, they can count on institutional channels to keep French alive throughout the country. Despite some decline in the last few years, especially on the West Coast, French still is one of the most frequently taught foreign languages in American schools and colleges. In addition, the French government maintains some schools with a French curriculum in this country, as well as a network of institutions such as the Alliance Française whose primary goal is to disseminate knowledge of the French language and culture to the public at large. There are also parochial and other French or bilingual schools in a number of places.

This infrastructure is obviously a potential source of support for first-generation French immigrants who wish to transmit their linguistic heritage to later generations. However, it seems to be the case that they view language transmission mostly as a private undertaking to be carried out at the level of the family unit, rather than a collective task to be performed at other levels as well. We will, therefore, take the family as our frame of reference, mentioning formal mechanisms of language transmission (schooling in particular) only as needed.

Our starting point is the examination of French language skills in my respondents' offspring, with the main focus on the second generation. We then attempt to account for their degree of proficiency in French, which shows a great deal of variation, through a description of language transmission as a process conditioned by various objective and attitudinal factors.

French Language Skills in the Offspring of First-Generation Immigrants

The findings to be presented in this section are based on my semi-formal interviews with 73 respondents who are raising or have raised children in the United States. Other respondents in the total sample of 96 first-generation French immigrants either have no children (19 cases) or have children who lived in France until age 16 or older (4 cases).

These 73 respondents were asked to give an assessment of their children's current French language skills. Those with more than one child were to report on the first-born and the last-born in the family. Children under age six were excluded, since their reading and writing abilities could not receive a fair assessment. The total number of "children" under consideration here is 114. They range in age from 6 to 68 years; the fact that many of them are now adults is due to the deliberate age skewing in my selection of first-generation immigrants for participation in this study.

A five-point scale (Non-existent, Poor, Fair, Good, Excellent) was used for separate assessments of understanding, speaking, reading and writing (Items #39 and 40 in the Appendix). The computation of scores was done as follows: Non-existent = 0, Poor = 1, Fair = 2, Good = 3, Excellent = 4; a "perfect" score is 16.

Contrary to what happened in the case of first-generation individuals, I had few chances to do my own assessment of language skills in subsequent generations. However, my respondents' evaluation of their offspring's proficiency in French can probably be considered as reasonably accurate for a number of reasons. First of all, the relevant questions in the interview had a familiar format, since previous questions had addressed the respondents' own language skills. Second, when applicable, parents showed great care in distinguishing the degree of proficiency in a first-born and a last-born child in the family, often volunteering detailed comparisons. Finally, in the (few) cases in which I was in a position to make my own judgment, it corresponded rather closely to the respondent's assessment, especially regarding differences between siblings.

Table 7.4 shows the average overall proficiency score for all four French language skills in the 114 second-generation individuals to be 8.5, with a range of 16 to 0. Both "perfect scorers" (15 cases) and "zero scorers" (9 cases) cover a wide age range: They are 13 to 46 years old in the first case and 9 to 44 years old in the second case, which seems to indicate that age is not a significant predictor of their French language skills. On the other hand, sibling rank has a certain impact, as evidenced by a comparison of the 64 first-born or only children and the 50 last-born children. The average overall proficiency score for all four

Table 7.4
French Language Skills in the Second Generation

	Average overall proficiency score *	Inter-individual range
First-born or only children (N = 64)	10.0	16 - 0
Last-born children (N = 50)	7.1	16 - 0
Both types of children (N = 114)	8.5	16 - 0

*Perfect score =16

French language skills is 10.0 in the first case, 7.1 in the second case. Within each of the two categories, we find a great deal of individual variation, with scores ranging from 16 to zero; there are 11 "perfect scorers" and one "zero scorer" among the 64 first-born or only children, versus 4 perfect scorers and 2 zero scorers among the 50 last-born siblings. These findings parallel those of other researchers, such as Varro (1988) in her study of American women married to French men in Paris: In a family of several children, the eldest is likely to be the most skilled in the parental immigrant language.

Other individual scores clearly bring out different levels of proficiency in the various language skills: All second-generation individuals under consideration, regardless of sibling rank, have better skills in understanding and speaking French than they do in reading and writing it. Many other studies of bilingualism show similar results, for obvious reasons. The spoken language can be mastered fairly easily in a natural environment, such as a home with an active immigrant language. But reading and writing in the language take more of an effort, which the second generation may not be willing to make if there is insufficient motivation.

In subsequent generations, even the verbal skills are often absent. My semiformal interviews did not include any specific questions about language transmission past the second generation. However, 23 respondents provided information, either spontaneously or as a result of probing questions on my part, about the French language skills of their grandchildren and, in one case, great-grandchildren. Given the unsystematic nature of this part of my data collection, the findings must be considered as tentative. But they correspond to my long-term observations of French immigrants and their descendants on the West Coast, which can be summarized as follows: Retention of the French language is practically nil past the second generation.

Among the 77 grandchildren and 8 great-grandchildren for whom I have language information, only 3 third-generation individuals (ages 3, 12, and 31 respectively) can qualify as fluent speakers of French. For all others, French language skills range from limited (6 cases) to practically or totally nonexistent (68 cases). None of the 8 fourth-generation individuals knows any French, which their great-grandmother laments, attributing it to a lack of motivation in her offspring.

Many factors converge to create such a situation, leaving unfulfilled the dream of some French-born individuals to initiate their children, grandchildren, and great-grandchildren to French. Isolated immigrants, even more than those who have the support of an ethnic community, face an enormous challenge when attempting to transmit their language of origin, a challenge that begins at home.

The Process of Language Transmission Within the Family

This section begins with a brief account of family configuration as a factor of variation in the process of language transmission. We then turn to a description of patterns of language use within the family, both at home and in public: Who speaks what to whom and in what circumstances? Finally, the establishment and maintenance of home bilingualism is shown to be strongly influenced by attitudinal factors.

Family Configuration as a Factor of Variation

Previous studies of bilingualism have isolated a number of variables that have a particularly strong impact on language maintenance within the family, one of them being sibling rank. We saw earlier that my findings confirm those of many other researchers: First-born or only children are usually more proficient in a parental foreign language than last-born siblings. Generally speaking, the parents' influence tends to be less strong on the younger children in a family. On the other hand, an older sibling may have a direct or an indirect influence on a younger sibling's language learning, as pointed out by several participants in my study.

> My daughter switched to English at age 3. So when her brother was born two years later, there was no French spoken in our home any longer.

Table 7.5
French Language Skills in Children of Mononational versus Mixed Couples

	Average overall proficiency score*	Inter-individual range
Children of mononational couples (N = 10)	12.6	16 - 0
Children of mixed couples (N=40)	8.4	16 - 0

*Perfect score = 16

> The switch to English in our family was mostly due to our son. At age 5, when his sister was born, he did not want to speak French any longer. So I did not raise my second child in French.

Another strong predictor of language maintenance is the nature of the parental couple (mononational versus mixed). In order to isolate this factor of variation, I built a subsample of second-generation individuals in which sibling rank has been eliminated as a variable. This subsample consists of 50 first-born or only children whose parents are either both French (10 cases) or one French and one American (40 cases). All 50 children are six years of age or older; all were born and are/were raised in the United States or, if born elsewhere, came to this country before age three and have lived here for a number of years. The narrowing of criteria, combined with the limited number of all-French couples in my larger sample, prevented me from having an equal number of children in each of the two categories (mononational versus mixed parental couple) in this subsample.

It seems reasonable to assume that a mononational couple will find it easier than a linguistically mixed couple to transmit an immigrant language to their children. This assumption is borne out by my data, as shown in Table 7.5.

- In the 10 first-born or only children of mononational couples, the average overall proficiency score for all four French language skills is 12.6; the range is from a perfect score of 16 for half the children, to zero for one of them.
- In the 40 first-born or only children of mixed couples, the average total score is 8.4; the range is from a perfect score of 16 for one-tenth of the children, to zero for two of them.

Table 7.6
French Language Skills in Children of Mixed Couples in Relation to the American Parent's Knowledge of French

	Average overall proficiency score*	Inter-individual range
Children whose American parent has excellent knowledge of French (N=8)	10.7	16 – 4
Children whose American parent has no knowledge of French (N=7)	4.0	16 - 0

*Perfect score = 16

While the figures go in the expected direction, they do not reveal as large a difference between the two categories of children as might have been anticipated. We need to refine our index of French language proficiency by considering another variable, namely the French language skills of the American spouses in the mixed couples.

As in the case of their children, non-French spouses were rated by the respondents for understanding, speaking, reading, and writing in French along a 5-point scale, from Non-existent to Excellent (Item #8 in the Appendix). Table 7.6 shows the average overall proficiency score for all four French skills in the 40 American spouses to be 8.3; individual scores range from 16 (eight cases) to zero (seven cases). In the eight families in which the American parent has excellent knowledge of French (16), the average score for French language skills in the child is 10.7, with an inter-individual range of 16 to 4. In the seven families in which the American spouse has no knowledge of French at all, the average score for French language skills in the child is 4.0, with an interindividual range of 16 to zero. It therefore seems to be the case that the American parent's knowledge of the immigrant language has an impact on the children's abilities in that language.

Patterns of Language Use at Home and in Public

It should be noted at the outset that, in the case of French immigrants, family bilingualism is a matter of choice. Since the immigrant generation usually comes with a knowledge of English and often continues to improve it after immigration, the second generation does not have to speak French at home out of necessity—barring an occasional visit by French relatives who may not be proficient in English. We should therefore expect family language planning to require a certain amount of control on the parents' part, calling for the use of specific strategies, especially once the child grows older.

Home bilingualism often begins in a rather spontaneous, noncontrived manner. Foreign-born parents may find it both easier and more pleasant to speak to an infant in their native language. In fact, they may know nursery rhymes and songs only in that language, which would naturally lead to a generalized use of it with a young child. Depending on circumstances, the child may be "sheltered" from English for a while, getting a good foundation in the parental immigrant language. Sooner or later, however, the child's exposure to English will become a major factor in the maintenance of the immigrant language within the family, often leading to fluctuation in the process of language transmission.

We will now examine this process within the time perspective of a family's child-rearing stage, from the time when the children are born to the time when they "leave the nest." My analysis is based on the subsample of 50 families (headed by 10 mononational and 40 mixed couples) described in the previous section. The data consist of answers to several interview questions dealing with the dynamics of language use between members of the family, both at home and in public. It was made clear to the respondents that they were to answer these questions in terms of either the present for those currently raising children or the past for those whose offpsring had reached adulthood. In the second case, respondents appeared to find it easy to recount specific details about the child-rearing stage of their lives, no matter how long ago it may have been.

The birth of a first child in a family headed by one or two foreign-born parent(s) can be the occasion for conscious parental decisions regarding language use: Is the child going to be first exposed only to English, only to the immigrant language, or both? In the event that the second or third solution is chosen, a question of tactics will often arise: Who will speak what language to the child? My respondents' answers to Question #27 in the interview provide the following picture for the 50 families under consideration: In almost two-thirds (33) of them, the eldest or only child in the family learned French as a first language, either by itself (21 cases) or concurrently with English (12 cases).

This is a rather promising picture of transmission of the French language: Only approximately one-third (17) of the 50 children in this subsample did not learn French as a first language. However, the simple strategy of addressing a baby or an infant in an immigrant language does not necessarily lead to a high level of proficiency in that language later in life, since many circumstances may or may not be under the control of immigrant parents.

One stage at which parental decisions and tactics can be of crucial importance is the beginning of school attendance for children. Unless they are sent to schools in which the immigrant language has its place, they will be constantly exposed to English; in addition, the onset of peer pressure may lead them to partial or total rejection of a home language that makes them feel different. A number of participants in my study whose children learned French as a first language, either exclusively or concurrently with English, report abrupt changes of course at that particular stage. In the two instances presented earlier, in which children suddenly switched to English at ages three and five respectively, the change was directly linked to the beginning of school attendance. Incidentally, the parents may be the ones initiating the switch to English at that point.

> I spoke only French to my two children until the older one turned five. When she started school I began speaking English to her, and in two months, both children forgot all of their French.

An obvious solution to the problem would be to send the children to a French-medium school, but this is not a common strategy among first-generation French immigrants. The subsample of 50 families under consideration only contains six cases of present or past attendance at a French or bilingual school (five of them in the Los Angeles area, and one in the San Francisco Bay area). Granted that such institutions are far and few in the Pacific region, particularly in nonmetropolitan areas, it seems to be the case that French-born parents often do not even entertain the idea of patronizing them, as attested by some of my respondents's answers to Question #57 in the interview.

The reasons they enumerated (with multiple responses in some cases) for not sending their children to a French-speaking school fall into three categories:

- lack of availability; this response was chosen by approximately two-thirds of the respondents, including some who live or who had lived within commuting distance of such schools in the San Francisco Bay or Los Angeles area—several of whom commented that they "just never thought about it."

- financial considerations; only one-fifth of the respondents chose this response, which is not surprising since many of them have/had the means to pay for school tuition, and there are opportunities for scholarships in French schools in the United States.

- personal choice; this response was chosen by approximately one-fourth of the respondents, some of whom made specific comments about their decision not to use this strategy for language transmission:

> I considered sending my children to a French school [in Los Angeles], but my [American] husband would not have supported the idea.

> I would possibly have done it when they were very young if it had been available, but not later, because I personally think that the ideal is French at home and English at school.

This particular stance, which is common among first-generation French immigrants, puts a heavy burden on the family unit for implementing bilingualism. In the absence of geographically defined French communities, as well as after-school or weekend French language programs for children, parents who do not send their children to French-speaking schools are almost entirely responsible for language transmission. Given their relatively low level of interest in organizational and community activities, as discussed earlier (Chapter 5), we should not expect them to count on others for helping their children learn and retain the French language. Participants in my study fit the pattern that I have observed for many years: French immigrants in the United States seem to consider bilingualism as a "family affair," rather than a collective undertaking.

So we need to examine their daily patterns of language use in order to understand the process of language transmission: Who speaks what to whom and when? Several questions in my semiformal interviews (Items #32–35 and 37–38 in the Appendix) elicited information on the frequency of use of French and English, at home and in public, in various combinations of family members at home or in public (for example, parents to children, or children to siblings) with special attention to the French parents' linguistic behavior.

There is no question that the beginning of school attendance has a decisive influence on the process of language retention in the second generation, since many children switch to exclusive use of English at that point. However, one or both parents may continue to address them in French, a strategy that creates asymmetrical patterns of language use within the family.

> Our daughter started speaking English at home at age six, when she started going to school. But I never stopped speaking French to her, even though my [French] husband started answering her in English.

> My children [ages seven and nine, respectively] understand French, but they don't want to speak it any longer. They answer in English even when I speak French to them.

Some parents develop interesting strategies, trying to reach linguistic compromises, but children may not want to go along with such tactics, despite possible immediate consequences. One respondent used to have a designated day of the week for the family to speak French over dinner; she reports that one day her son (then age nine) refused to conform and, when given the choice to speak French or leave the table, opted for the second solution.

During the teenage and early adolescence years, when children are particularly prone to rebel against parental influence and want to conform to the peer group, their use of French is likely to decline even further.

> My teenage children are reluctant to speak French because they've had to suffer from other kids for being different. My daughter started making negative remarks about French at age twelve.

> At that age, kids want to belong . . . I once brought back good bikes from France for my two sons, but they never used them because they were different from their friends' bikes. I also sent each of them twice to France, separately, for a whole year. They stayed with my parents and went to school there. But every time one of them returned from France, he immediately drifted back to English.

Self-consciousness can also occur in late adolescence and "undo" the work of many years, sometimes beyond repair despite parental efforts.

> We always spoke French in our home, since my husband was French too. But at age 17, my third child stopped speaking French

because he thought it looked "sissy," and he's never wanted to speak
it since then.

By the time the children leave the nest, the proficiency they may still
have in the French language is more likely than ever to disappear,
especially in the (extremely frequent) case of outmarriage.

Sometimes I call him and speak French to him if he is alone, and
he answers in English. It has been like that ever since he got married, because his wife does not speak French.

But intermarriage is only one factor that, incidentally, does not always operate, as attested by the following instance. One respondent
has a daughter married to a French man and a son married to an American, all of whom live in the United States. His two grandsons in the
first household (one of whom was actually born in France) have limited
skills in French, whereas his 12-year-old grandson in the second household is one of the only three third-generation fluent speakers of French
in my sample at large.

The discontinuance of bilingualism can also result from relocation or
the general demands of a young adult's life. This is particularly true
when grandparents are the "promoters" of language transmission,
since there may be fewer and fewer chances for visits. One respondent
whose granddaughter is currently fluent in French, thanks mostly to
daily conversations between the two of them, fears that the situation
will change drastically, now that this 31-year-old woman (another of
the three fluent third-generation speakers of French in my sample) has
moved away to a new job. Other respondents who had acted, at one
time or another, as active transmitters of the French language to the
third generation, lament the negative outcome of their efforts. Two of
them had raised their respective granddaughters for several years,
speaking French to them all the time; some had taken grandchildren
along on extended visits with French-speaking relatives in France or
helped high school age grandchildren with their French classes. In
most cases, these strategies have failed to lead to permanent results;
as soon as contact becomes less regular between the two generations,
the young people forget their French. Obviously, the dynamics of
everyday language use play a crucial role in the transmission of a linguistic heritage.

Let us return to the second generation and examine linguistic be-

Table 7.7
Use of the French Language within the Family at Home and in Public

	Always %	Usually %	Sometimes %	Never %
At home				
French parents to children	14	20	40	26
Children to French parents	10	12	28	50
Parents alone	20	0	12	68
Both parents to children	16	0	18	66
Children to American parents	0	0	10	90
Children to siblings	2	0	15	83
In public				
French parents to children	12	10	28	50
Both parents to children	8	0	20	72

havior within the family during their childhood years, focusing on the frequency of use of the French language at home or in public. The following analysis is based on the same subsample of 50 families as above (10 of them headed by all-French couples and 40 by mixed couples), except that the pattern of inter-sibling language use is based on 41 cases only because there are nine families with one child each.

The following is a summary of the patterns emerging from the data, as shown in Table 7.7.

At home:

• French parents speak French to their children when alone with them in 74 percent of all cases, including 34 percent who always or usually do so, and 40 percent sometimes.

• Children speak French to the French parent(s) in 50 percent of all cases, including 22 percent who always or usually do so and 28 percent sometimes.

• French parents speak French with their (French or American) spouses when alone with them in 32 percent of all cases, including 20 percent who always do so and 12 percent sometimes.

• French parents and their (French or American) spouses speak French to their children in 34 percent of all cases, including 16 percent who always do so and 18 percent sometimes.

• Children speak French to an American parent at home in 10 percent of all cases, on a "sometimes" basis.

- Children speak French to siblings at home in 17 percent of all applicable cases (nonapplicable: nine cases of only children), including 2 percent who always do so and 15 percent sometimes.

In public:

- French parents speak French to their children when "alone" with them in 50 percent of all cases, including 22 percent who always or usually do so and 28 percent sometimes.
- French parents and their (French or American) spouses speak French to their children in 28 percent of all cases, including 8 percent who always do so and 20 percent sometimes.

These patterns reveal some general trends that account in part for the moderate level of retention of the French language past the first generation:

- A majority (three-quarters) of the French parents speak French to their children at least part of the time when alone with them at home, but this strategy does not create reciprocal patterns: in only half of the cases do the children speak French to these French parents at least part of the time.
- The impact of intermarriage is confirmed: The children's use of French at home decreases considerably when they speak to an American parent, rather than their French parents.
- The strong impact of siblings is also confirmed: French is hardly ever used for communication between children within the family. It has to be attributed in large part to the fact that the children of first-generation French immigrants are usually surrounded by English-speaking playmates.
- Being in public lowers the use of French by parents speaking to their children, even in the case of French parents "alone" with them. Some respondents report that when they speak French in public, their children get embarrassed.

This last remark brings us close to psychological determinants of language use within the family. It is understandable that, for reasons of politeness or due to possible embarrassment for the children, some French parents would not use the same strategies in public as they do at home. It is more difficult to account for the total or partial lack of French speaking at home in a sizable proportion of the households under consideration, given the general picture we gave earlier of the respondents' strong attachment to their linguistic heritage. Particularly puzzling are the (few) cases of children of mononational (French + French) couples whose knowledge of French is limited or nonexistent—until we delve into the parents' motives for acting the way they do/did. As in the case of other immigrant populations, parental attitudes seem to play an important role in language transmission among the French in the United States.

Parental Attitudes Toward Bilingualism

At a theoretical level, most participants in this study appear to be in favor of the preservation of the French language through family bilingualism, as evidenced by their answers to the following question (Item #71 in the Appendix): "In your opinion, is it important for French people in the United States to have their children learn the French language?" An overwhelming majority of 73 respondents out of 96 answered positively without any reservations, 14 responded positively with some reservations, and 5 answered negatively; the remaining 4 were undecided.

Those who answered positively without any reservations give the following arguments in favor of bilingualism:

- intellectual and practical advantages of knowing several languages, especially in today's world: "an incredible gift to your child," or "a mind-opening experience."
- the need for their children to "feel that French connection," keep their roots, be able to understand their parents' background, and also to communicate with people in France, particularly their relatives.
- the necessity of preserving "the precious French heritage."

Some interesting points are made by those who see it as important for French people in the United States to have their children learn French but have some reservations about it:

- It is a difficult, sometimes impossible task, particularly "if only one parent insists on it."

- It depends on a number of circumstances, such as place of residence or the parents' lifestyle: "It makes less sense in a small town, because there are no opportunities to practice."
- It is a personal choice, for instance, "it depends on how much you want your children to adapt to the United States."
- The extent and timing of it should be left up to the individuals concerned: "It does not have to be right away; once the children master English, it would help them to learn French, since there are so many French words in English."

Finally, for the five individuals who do not think that it is important for French people in the United States to have their children learn the French language, there are two types of arguments: deterioration of the French language and advocacy of a *laissez faire* attitude:

> It is not important because the French are not as proud of their language as they used to be, and they are more willing to speak English.

> It does not really matter; if the children want to learn it, fine, but if not, that's OK too.

This last point reminds us of the importance of personal choice in the lives of French immigrants in the United States. They tend to project this dimension of life onto their children. When asked (Item #36 in the Appendix) how strict they are/were regarding the use of the French language by their children at home, only 5 of the 50 respondents under consideration report being/having been very or rather strict about it; most of the remaining 45 respondents exert(ed) no pressure at all.

As for the specific reasons (Question #43 in the Appendix) why some of them did not initiate or maintain the use of strategies fostering family bilingualism, they can be rather vague:

> There is no particular reason why we stopped speaking French at home, it just was not very practical.

In most cases, however, respondents have a clear picture of the reasons why bilingualism never was, or ceased to be, part of their family lives. Some confess to "laziness" (their own term) or evoke pragmatic reasons such as lack of time or disruptive family moves. Others recognize that their exclusive use of English is/was self-serving, being based on their need to learn/practice English; such was the case, in particular, for an all-French couple whose three children, now adults, have absolutely no knowledge of French.

A few respondents stress the need to have children exercise free choice regarding language use.

> I did not want to push my children one way or the other.

> When I was raising my children, there were kids in the neighborhood who resented having to speak their parents' language at home, rather than English. So I wanted my own children to choose, and that meant *not* speaking French to them at first, when they could have been influenced so easily.

Others point to their spouses' lack of proficiency in French as the main factor in their decision to avoid or discontinue the use of French at home.

> My wife knew almost no French. At first I tried to speak French to the children, but it just did not work out.

> My husband did not know French. I tried to raise my children bilingually, but it was a real effort to keep it up, just by myself.

Most important, however, are parental attitudes toward bilingualism *per se*, which may be one-sided in a mixed couple.

> My husband basically supports my idea of speaking French at home, but deep down he thinks that we should speak French only when we are in France.

> At first my [French] mother lived with us, so we spoke a lot of French. But then she moved out of our home, and by the time our second child was born, my husband wanted only English in our home.

Strong spousal opposition to the use of French in their homes may extend beyond the family.

> My husband was always offended when we had visitors from France who could not speak English. It made him even more resistant to bilingualism for our children.

Such attitudes in non-French spouses are occasionally grounded in negative past experiences.

> My husband was not in favor of bilingualism because he was raised in a German-Dutch colony in Illinois, and sometimes he was put to shame because of his English.

> My wife was *pushed* to learn French while growing up in New Hampshire, because she is of French-Canadian ancestry. She technically *hated* it, so she does *not* want that kind of pressure on our kids.

A few of the respondents have negative attitudes toward bilingualism that may be grounded in fears of harming the children.

> I first spoke French to my daughter, but by age three she started having nightmares dreaming of words in the two languages. So we stopped speaking French at home.

> With only one parent in the family knowing French, I was afraid that it might confuse the child to go back and forth between the two languages.

Such fears are sometimes based on misconceptions regarding cognitive development and particularly language learning.

> Personally I see the use of French at home as an obstacle to learning English well, so I did not want to take a chance with my children.

> I wanted my sons to learn only English so that they would not be confused. Frankly, I think that bilingualism is more negative than positive, unless English is first and the other language secondary.

> I am not in favor of bilingualism because it means not knowing either language well. I did not raise my son in French, and as a result [*sic*] he was an A student in English.

One respondent recognizes that she had "bad advice from teachers who were against bilingualism." Another one evokes the general negative attitudes toward bilingualism at the time (1960s) when she was raising a family. Obviously even speakers of French, whose language is held in high esteem in the United States, may bend to social or individual pressures that discourage family bilingualism.

Parental attitudes toward bilingualism can also play an important role in language transmission past the second generation. A number of respondents report having been thwarted in their efforts to transmit the French language to their grandchildren, most often by an in-law who feels negative about it. In one case, a nine year old had asked her grandmother to teach her French, and the grandmother was about to joyfully embark on this venture, but she confided in me that her son's American wife was "not excited about it, to say the least." Negative attitudes toward bilingualism may be compounded by somewhat conflictual relationships between generations, as in the following case.

> My daughter married an American who does not know French and thinks that one must speak English in the United States. Their daughter knows almost no French. I've tried to speak French to her when she visits me alone, but she is resisting. And anyway, I've had to learn to stay in my place regarding my granddaughter's education.

This picture of parental attitudes toward bilingualism and their consequences on the transmission of a linguistic heritage underlines, once more, the significance of personal choice in the lives of French immigrants in the United States. Variability in retention of the French language past the first generation has been shown to be conditioned by a number of objective factors, such as family configuration and the general dynamics of family life, reminding us that intent is not sufficient for a language to be maintained through the generations. We also stressed the importance of individual decision making in matters such as schooling for the children in an immigrant population that, overall, can *choose* its degree of ethnicity in the American context.

LANGUAGE AS A MARKER OF ETHNICITY

Can the French language be regarded as a marker of ethnicity in the case of French immigrants in the United States? One interview question (Item #69 in the Appendix) directly addressed this issue: "Do you think that it is possible to remain French without speaking French?" Almost half of the 93 respondents who answered the question regard the French language as an essential component of "Frenchness"; they think that it is absolutely impossible to remain French without speaking French. The link between language and ethnicity is obvious for them, as indicated by some strongly worded answers that reveal a keen sense of the centrality of language in ethnic identification.

> No, you can't remain French without speaking French. Language has *so* much to do with one's identity!

> Impossible. Someone who does not speak French any longer is no longer French.

> No, I would not consider people as French if they did not speak French any longer, even if they wore bérets.

Among the other 49 respondents, 18 show a certain degree of uncertainty, wavering back and forth between abstract generalizations and personal reactions.

> I guess in a sense it's possible to remain French without speaking French. But if I focus on a particular person, I'd say that it may not be possible after all. I would have trouble accepting him as French if he spoke no French at all.

> Technically it's possible, but I don't see how one can keep the cultural values without speaking the language any longer.

The 31 remaining responses, however, tend to be categorical, as if there were absolutely no doubt in the respondents' minds about the separability of language and ethnic identification.

> Sure, you *can* remain French without speaking French.

> I know a case like that, a French couple that has lived here for over 40 years, they are as French as can be, but they always speak English, even to each other.

In a few cases, the role of language is seen as overshadowed by the significance of national origins or birthplace in the definition of ethnicity.

> Oh yes, you can remain French without speaking French because it's in your heart. If you were born French, even if you never speak it, you are still French.

If you were born in France where French is the language, even if you don't speak it any longer, you are still French in spirit.

Strikingly absent from the respondents' comments, even when they give a central place to language in ethnic identification, are references to the French language as a bond between French immigrants at a general level, or as a marker of group boundaries. Only one respondent alludes to a sense of membership based on language, and he focuses on merely individual aspects of it.

Maybe one can remain French without speaking French, but it's difficult. Feeling close to somebody of the same nation disappears if you forget the language.

The same emphasis on the individual, rather than a collective entity, emerges from my respondents' answers to another question in the interview (Item #70 in the Appendix) regarding the best ways for them to retain their language of origin. Their responses demonstrate that they rely mostly on individual actions for that purpose. For an overwhelming majority of them (84 out of 96), reading French books or periodicals is a major instrument of language retention; there are also frequent references to films and television, trips to France, and regular telephone conversations with friends and relatives in France. While almost two-thirds of the respondents say that one of the best ways for them to retain French is to speak it, fewer than one in seven mentions contacts with co-ethnics or participation in French organizations and activities in the United States as means to that end.

The predominantly individual character of their language maintenance severely limits the role of French as a marker of ethnicity. The use of an immigrant language in the household is significant in itself, but it does not automatically create a "field of communication and interaction" that could serve to define a group in Barth's sense of the term (Barth 1969: 11). In the absence of a sufficient role at the societal level, the French language makes only a limited contribution to the formation of a collective identity among French immigrants in the United States.

Conclusion

French people who live here are a strange breed. . . . They remain
very French in many ways, but in spite of that, they do not constitute a close community, as other ethnic groups do. They seem to be
too individualistic to have the necessary *esprit de corps*. Besides,
most of the French people here are well educated, so it seems that
they are better equipped to blend into American society without
losing their own identity.

This self-reflective image, contributed by a participant in my study,
appropriately encapsulates the present situation of the French population in the United States. As I initially contended on the basis of my
own insider's perspective, French immigrants do not really constitute
an ethnic group on the contemporary American scene. This observation
has now been validated by the results of an investigation grounded in
ethnographic methods of inquiry. Some of the major findings of my
descriptive study are recapitulated here, within the broad perspective
of acculturation in immigrant populations.

French-born individuals who have settled in the United States in
recent times hardly fit the traditional "immigrant paradigm." Their
motives for emigration are most often personal in nature; economic

factors only play a limited role, and political or religious factors practically none, in their decision to depart from France. Many of them come
singly to this country, without any support from co-ethnic networks,
others emigrate with an American spouse they met overseas, or more
exceptionally as a mononational (French) family. In any of these cases,
their transition from France to the United States is often facilitated by
some prior knowledge of English.

Once they settle in this country, first-generation French immigrants
for the most part live among non-French people. Those who become
permanent immigrants tend to achieve high levels of education and
occupational status due only in part to their social origins; other factors
are a highly developed sense of self-direction and the motivation to
achieve through hard work. These social characteristics converge with
a notably high intermarriage rate to make the French perfect candidates for fast integration into American society—a process that, generally speaking, has been accelerating throughout the twentieth
century because of increasing societal pressures for uniformization. "A
pervasive American culture, functioning through schools, media, consumerism, and the expectation expressed that newcomers will adopt
the civic culture, has posed great challenges for groups struggling
for a balance between cultural preservation and cultural adaptation"
(Barkan 1999: 13).

For contemporary French immigrants, this balancing act between
attachment to one's origins and adaptation to American society is a
predominantly individual, rather than collective, undertaking because
of a number of structural and attitudinal factors. The current French
population in the United States is numerically insignificant and has no
territorial identity, given its scattered geographical distribution and
the absence of spatially defined communities populated by direct immigrants from France. It has a low degree of institutional identity
grounded in a weak religious, educational, and political infrastructure,
and there seems to be a growing lack of interest among more recent
French immigrants in such formal support for ethnicity.

French organizational life in the United States centers mostly
around the promotion of French language and culture in the public at
large, rather than the establishment of solidarity bonds between co-
ethnics—a situation that seems to fit the needs of present-day French
immigrants, who are not strongly inclined to join associations. Consequently, there is no tangible ethnic community for most French-born
individuals who are permanently settled in this country.

It might be argued that they have an "imaginary" community, being united by common national origins, a common cultural and linguistic heritage, and a partially shared cognitive model of their dual world—as attested by my empirical data. However, this community is distinctly cultural in nature, rather than ethnic: It is fashioned by a French identity that has its roots in the "old country," rather than the new one. Common manifestations of this French identity in the foreign-born generation are a very high level of native language retention, maintenance of some cultural traditions in their homes, and the use of various strategies (for instance, regular reading of French periodicals and frequent visits to the homeland) to remain in contact with the French world. In addition, my analysis of some perceptual dimensions of ethnicity has revealed the existence, in the minds of first-generation French immigrants, of a model of their dual world suggesting that they "behave as Americans, but deep down remain very French," as remarked by a participant in my study.

This identification of the foreign-born generation with a distant homeland, rather than a local French community in the United States, makes it difficult for subsequent generations to maintain a French identity. The "missing link" is a new, hybrid identity partaking of both Frenchness and Americanness, forged through regular interaction with co-ethnics. The importance of such exposure for the preservation of ethnic identity has been noted by an observer of French-speaking Canadians in Toronto, a population that "exemplifies almost total participation outside of ethnic boundaries within the English-speaking host population," the end result being "alternative identifications which weaken and dissolve ethnic identity" (Maxwell 1977: 137).

Interestingly, a comparable situation seems to prevail among Americans who are permanently settled in Europe, as noted in the Introduction to a collection of articles dealing with their acculturation. "Americans with European spouses living in Europe often have little to do with the American communities in their respective countries. They are members of local families" (Varro and Boyd 1998: 18). The marriage factor converges with other social and contextual factors to influence the transmission of their heritage to their children. Those who are married to local nationals in particular tend to have children who, while they may be bilingual, are dominant in the local language because of its use in public, at school, and sometimes in the home.

Such language dominance patterns have often been shown, in studies of bilingualism, to lead to partial or total loss of the parental foreign language past adolescence. According to a recent overview of ethnic groups in the United States, "immigrants have sought to preserve traditional language use, while the children have been far less committed to language retention, just as homeland issues have less salience for them. Except for physically isolated groups and those where the language maintenance is inseparable from the maintenance of religion, language shift has invariably occurred by the second and certainly by the third generation" (Barkan 1999: 13).

The maintenance of a parental foreign language appears to be a challenge even in populations with exceptionally high concentrations, such as speakers of Spanish in some parts of the country. A survey of the current situation in Miami shows that, while home language retention is very high in Latin American groups, especially among students of Cuban origin who attend private schools, English language dominance is practically unavoidable. "Second-generation youth not only report widespread competence in English, but also demonstrate an unambiguous preference for it in everyday communication. Children raised in the core of the Spanish-speaking Miami community (those attending bilingual private schools) are actually the most enthusiastic in their preference for the language of the land" (Portes and Schauffler 1996: 442).

In the case of the French, a population consisting of isolated immigrants in this country, the temptation is very strong for second-generation youth to (totally or partially) abandon the language of their foreign-born parents, particularly in the absence of support for continued bilingualism beyond the family. An immigrant language that is used only in the home will likely die a natural death if not supported by outside means. Some first-generation French immigrants seem to assume that their own retention of the French language and their efforts to implement its use in the home, complemented by extended family visits to France, should be sufficient to ensure continued bilingualism in their offspring. Unfortunately, this goal cannot be reached easily without a certain level of institutional or organizational support, as well as sustained interaction with co-ethnics in the United States.

Such a course of action is a challenge for an immigrant population characterized by a high level of social integration in this country. Many factors converge to hinder the transmission of the French heritage to later generations, including the strong desire of French-born parents to see their offspring well integrated in American society. This attitude on their part accounts for their increasing use, as their children grow up, of adaptive and accommodative strategies in the private and public sphere, in order to strike a balance between cultural preservation and cultural adaptation. Theoretically, such patterns should not preclude the maintenance of a cultural and linguistic heritage, since acculturation can be additive rather than subtractive. However, the lack of cohesiveness within the current French population in this country makes it extremely difficult to counter the pressures of the surrounding society.

There is another dimension to this dilemma: the crucial role of personal decisions in the way people conduct their lives, particularly in the case of a population for which ethnicity is a matter of choice. In an article aptly entitled "Optional Ethnicities: For Whites Only?", Waters (1996) underlines the privileged position of descendants of Europeans in the United States, as compared to people with non-European origins. Some of her remarks, which are based on research among later-generation individuals of European ancestry, apply to French immigrants of both the first and subsequent generations, who can easily be co-opted by American society.

> Symbolic ethnicity is the best of all worlds for these respondents. These White ethnics can claim to be unique and special, while simultaneously finding the community and conformity with others that they also crave. But that "community" is of a type that will not interfere with a person's individuality. It is not as if these people belong to ethnic voluntary organizations or gather as a group in churches or neighborhoods or union halls. They work and reside within the mainstream of American middle-class life, yet they retain the interesting benefits—the "specialness"—of ethnic allegiance, without any of its drawbacks. (Waters 1996: 448–49)

This description of an intangible community corresponds, to a large extent, to the picture of contemporary French immigrants in the United States emerging from my findings. Particularly important is the strong sense of self-direction that characterizes this population. We should never lose sight of the fact that, for many contemporary French-born individuals who emigrated to the United States, the decision to undertake this *grand voyage* was an act of self-determination. Those who have stayed in this country strongly value individual freedom, personal choice, and sometimes even risk-taking. They are fortunate enough to originate from a country whose language and culture are, overall, highly regarded in the United States and the object of frequent attention. They are basically happy with their lives in this country, as long as they can remain French beneath the surface of social integration.

It should not come as a surprise that these first-generation immigrants from France tend to raise their children in the same independent mode that propelled them to the United States: Life should be a personal construction, marked by freedom of choice as much as possible. Such an attitude obviously has an impact on the maintenance of a French identity in the offspring of the foreign-born generation. Some members of the second generation choose to retain elements of the French language and culture past childhood and adolescence, others do not. But whatever their level of maintenance of the French linguistic and cultural heritage, they may retain what is perhaps the most precious part of the contemporary French immigrant experience: a sense of adventure, the desire to embark some day on a *grand voyage* that may change their lives forever.

Appendix: The Interview Guide

1. Place of birth
2. Date of birth
3. Present citizenship
4. When did you first come to the United States, and in what circumstances?
5. What is your marital status?
6. In what country was your spouse born?
7. Is/was your spouse a native speaker of French? If not, what is/was his/her native language?
8. If your spouse is/was not a native speaker of French, rate his/her skills in the French language.

	Understanding	Speaking	Reading	Writing
Non-existent				
Poor				
Fair				
Good				
Excellent				

9. What is the highest grade you completed in school? Do you have a professional or technical degree?

10. What is your occupation? If retired or unemployed, what was your occupation when you were working?

11. Which of these labels best characterizes the way you consider yourself at the present time?

American

French

French American

Other (Specify)

12. Have there been times or circumstances in your life when you have felt more American or more French? If so, please elaborate.

13. Have you changed your first or last name to make it sound more American? If so, please elaborate.

14. What ethnic group does each of your three closest friends in the USA belong to?

15. Besides your three closest friends, think of the other friends you have in the USA. How many of them are French?

None

Fewer than half

About half

More than half

16. Do you speak French (whenever possible) with your French friends in the USA?

Never

Sometimes

Always

17. What holidays do you celebrate in your home?

Only American holidays

Only French holidays

Both

Neither

18. In the case of holidays which are common to the USA and France, do you celebrate

The American way

The French way

In a "mixed" way

19. When you are at home, do you eat mostly

The American way
The French way
In a "mixed" way

20. How often do you go back to France?

Never
Sometimes
Frequently (Indicate frequency)

21. What language did you learn to speak first?
Do you presently consider it as your dominant language?

22. Rate your present skills in the French language.

	Understanding	Speaking	Reading	Writing
Poor				
Fair				
Good				
Excellent				

23. Rate your present skills in the English language.

	Understanding	Speaking	Reading	Writing
Poor				
Fair				
Good				
Excellent				

24. How often do you speak each of these languages at home?

	English	French	Other (Specify)
Never			
Sometimes			
Most of the time			
Always			

25. When you have a choice, what language do you prefer to use?

	English	French	Other (Specify)
At home			
Outside			

26. Please give the following information about your children.

	First name	Age	Gender	Country of birth
Oldest child				
Second child				
Third child				
Fourth child				
Fifth child				

27. What language did your children first learn to speak?

English

French

English and French at the same time

Other (Specify)

28. Of the stories, songs and nursery rhymes you use(d) for your children, do most belong to

The American tradition

The French tradition

Both about equally

29. How often do/did your children go (with you or alone) to France?

Never

Sometimes

Frequently (Indicate frequency)

30. Do/did you tell your children about the culture (history, music, literature, etc.) of France?

31. Do/did you try to keep your children informed of what is/was going on politically and/or socially in France?

32. What language do/did you speak to your children at home when alone with them?

	Always	Usually	Sometimes	Never
English				
French				
Other (Specify)				

33. What language do/did you speak to your children in public when "alone" with them?

	Always	Usually	Sometimes	Never
English				
French				
Other (Specify)				

34. Which language do/did you and your spouse generally speak

- when alone together
- when both with the children at home
- when both with the children in a public place

35. What language do/did your children speak to you at home when alone with you?

	Always	Usually	Sometimes	Never
English				
French				
Other (Specify)				

36. If you always speak/spoke French to your children at home when alone with them, how strict are/were you about their use of French to speak to you?

Very strict

Rather strict

Not very strict

No pressure exerted

37. What language do/did your children speak to your spouse at home?

	Always	Usually	Sometimes	Never
English				
French				
Other (Specify)				

38. What language do/did your children speak among themselves at home?

	Always	Usually	Sometimes	Never
English				
French				
Other (Specify)				

39. Rate your oldest child's present skills in French.

	Understanding	Speaking	Reading	Writing
Non-existent				
Poor				
Fair				
Good				
Excellent				

40. Rate your youngest child's present skills in French.

	Understanding	Speaking	Reading	Writing
Non-existent				
Poor				
Fair				
Good				
Excellent				

41. Are/were you consciously trying to raise your children bilingually?

Yes

No

Not really

42. If you are/were raising your children bilingually, can you state your reasons and also indicate your spouse's opinion in this matter?

43. If you are/were not raising your children bilingually, can you state your reasons? Also indicate if you started in the direction of bilingualism but stopped, and why.

44. If your children used to speak French but now refuse to speak it, can you state the reasons you think they may have and give an approximate date for the change?

45. Do you think that your children feel

More American than French

More French than American

A blend of the two

46. How many voluntary organizations in the USA do you belong to? How many of them are French? (You may list them if you prefer.)

	Total number of organizations	Total number of French organizations
Compatriotic societies		
Political organizations		
Charitable organizations		

	Total number of organizations	Total number of French organizations
Cultural organizations		
Sports organizations		
Choirs or dance ensembles		
Scholarly associations		
Professional associations		
Student associations		
Church committees		
Other (Specify)		

47. Have you in the last year or so assumed any position of responsibility in any of these non-French or French organizations? Please specify.

48. How often do you attend meetings of French voluntary organizations in the USA?

Never

Rarely

Sometimes

Frequently (Indicate frequency)

If Never or Rarely, is it due to

Lack of opportunity in your local community

Lack of time and/or money

Your own preference

Some other reason(s) (Specify)

49. In the last 12 months, how many of the following activities sponsored by French organizations did you attend in the USA?

	Times attended (in last 12 months)				
	0	1–2	3–5	6–10	11+
Musical concert					
Dance activity					
Art exhibit					
Bazaar/bake sale					
July 14 commemorations					
Lecture/panel discussion					
Picnic					

	0	1–2	3–5	6–10	11+
Theatrical event					
Party					
Other (Specify)					

If you had low attendance, is it due to

Lack of opportunity in your community

Lack of time and/or money

Your own preference

Some other reason(s) (Specify)

50. How often do you attend activities of non-French voluntary organizations in the USA?

Never

Rarely

Sometimes

Frequently (Indicate frequency)

If Never or Rarely, is it due to

Lack of opportunity in your local community

Lack of time and/or money

Your own preference

Some other reason(s) (Specify)

51. Which of the following public actions in the USA have you ever been involved in?

Getting jobs for other French people

Helping establish a French school

Furthering French interests in your local community

Other French-related actions (Specify)

52. Do you deal with French professionals (doctor, lawyer, accountant, etc.) in the USA? If so, specify what kind. Do you speak French with them whenever possible?

Never

Sometimes

Always

53. Have you patronized other places of business (gas station, store, etc.) mostly because they are French? If so, specify what kind. Do you speak French with them whenever possible?

Never

Sometimes

Always

54. Do you watch television programs in French in the USA?

Never

Sometimes

Frequently (Indicate frequency)

If Sometimes or Frequently, please list the exact programs.
55. Do you listen to radio programs in French in the USA?

Never

Sometimes

Frequently (Indicate frequency)

If Sometimes or Frequently, please list the exact programs.
56. Do you read French magazines or newspapers in the USA?

Never

Sometimes

Frequently (Indicate frequency)

If Sometimes or Frequently, please list the periodicals.
57. Do/did you send your children to a French day school?

No, because none is/was available nearby

No, because it is/was too expensive

No, because I do/did not want to

Yes

58. Do/did your children attend French cultural events in the USA?

Never

Sometimes

Frequently (Indicate frequency)

59. If you had a choice, in what country would you prefer to live just now?
60. Were there any aspects of France which you were glad to leave behind when you came to the USA? If so, please specify.

61. What do you like best about living in the USA?

62. What would you say you miss most, if anything, of France?

63. When you go to France, is it (You may check several answers.)

Because you must, for various reasons, but would just as soon go somewhere else

Mainly to see your family and friends in France

Mainly because you love being there again for a while

Other reasons (Specify)

64. Do you think that you would re-adapt to France if you were to go back there permanently?

Very easily

Rather easily

Not easily

65. Do you want your children to feel well integrated into American society?

Yes, very much

Yes

Not really

Not at all

66. Would you prefer/have preferred your children to marry

Americans

French people

Other (Specify)

Indifferent

67. Do you think Americans like

	Very much	Somewhat	Not at all
France as a country			
French people			
The French language			
The French culture			

68. How much prestige do you think the French language and culture have in the USA?

                              High   Medium   Low

The French language

The French culture

69. Do you think that it is possible to remain French without speaking French? Please elaborate.

70. What do you think are the best ways for you to retain the French language while living in the USA?

71. In your opinion is it important for French people in the USA to have their children learn the French language?

72. How important do you think it is for you to participate in French activities and organizations in the USA?

73. Please list ten adjectives which you associate with the French language.

74. Please list ten adjectives which you associate with American English.

75. What global images come to your mind when you think of the French language or France?

76. What global images come to your mind when you think of American English or the United States?

77. Please make a few personal statements about the French language of the kind "To me the French language is like . . ."

78. What do you think the place of the French language is in French culture and society?

79. Imagine for a moment that the French language and American English, or France and the United States, are protagonists in an encounter. How do you view each of them in this encounter?

80. Is there anything else you would like to say about French people in the United States?

Bibliography

Alba, Richard. *Ethnic Identity: The Transformation of White America*. New Haven, CT: Yale University Press, 1990.

Allen, James, and Eugene Turner. *We the People: An Atlas of America's Ethnic Diversity*. New York: Macmillan, 1988.

Bakalian, Amy. *Armenian-Americans: From Being to Feeling Armenian*. New Brunswick, NJ: Transaction Publishers, 1993.

Barkan, Elliott. *And Still They Come: Immigrants and American Society, 1920 to the 1990s*. Wheeling, IL: Harlan Davidson, 1996.

——— (ed.). *A Nation of Peoples. A Sourcebook on America's Multicultural Heritage*. Westport, CT: Greenwood Press, 1999.

Barrish, Gerald. *Ethnic Identification: The French in America*. Ph.D. thesis, University of Washington, 1992.

Barth, Frederik (ed.). *Ethnic Groups and Boundaries*. Boston: Little, Brown, 1969.

Blyth, Carl. "The Sociolinguistic Situation of Cajun French: The Effects of Language Shift and Language Loss." In Albert Valdman (ed.), *French and Creole in Louisiana*. New York: Plenum Press, 1997.

Buenker, John, and Lorman Ratner (eds.). *Multiculturalism in the United States: A Comparative Guide to Acculturation and Ethnicity*. Westport, CT: Greenwood Press, 1992.

Chavez, Leo. *Shadowed Lives: Undocumented Immigrants in American Society*. 2d ed. Orlando, FL: Harcourt, Brace, and Company, 1998.

Creagh, Ronald. *Nos cousins d'Amérique: Histoire des Français aux Etats-Unis.* Paris: Payot, 1988.

Douglass, William. "Basques." In Stephan Thernstrom, et al. (eds.), *Harvard Encyclopedia of American Ethnic Groups*, 173–179. Cambridge: Harvard University Press, 1980.

Fishman, Joshua. "Language and Ethnicity." In J. Edwards (ed.), *Linguistic Minorities, Policies and Pluralism*, 15–57. London: Academic Press, 1984.

———. *The Rise and Fall of the Ethnic Revival: Perspectives on Language and Ethnicity.* Berlin: Mouton, 1985.

Fohlen, Claude. "Perspectives historiques sur l'immigration française aux Etats-Unis." *Revue Européenne des Migrations Internationales*, 6, no. 1 (1990): 29–41.

Fouché, Nicole. *Emigration alsacienne aux Etats-Unis, 1815–1870.* Paris: Publications de la Sorbonne, 1992.

Foucrier, Annick. *Le rêve californien. Migrants français sur la côte Pacifique (XVIIIe–XXe siècles).* Paris: Belin, 1999.

Gans, Herbert. "Symbolic Ethnicity: the Future of Ethnic Groups and Cultures in America." *Ethnic and Racial Studies* 2 (1979): 1–20.

———. "Ethnicity, Ideology, and the Insider Problem." *Contemporary Sociology*, 14 (1985): 3.

Gauchey, Jacques. *La Vallée du Risque: Silicon Valley.* Paris: Plon, 1990.

Glazer, Nathan, and Daniel Moynihan. *Beyond the Melting Pot: The Negroes, Puerto Ricans, Jews, Italians and Irish of New York City.* Cambridge: MIT Press, 1963.

Gordon, Milton. *Assimilation in American Life: The Role of Race, Religion, and National Origins.* New York: Oxford University Press, 1964.

Gudykunst, William (ed.). *Language and Ethnic Identity.* Philadelphia, PA: Multilingual Matters, 1988.

Hall, Edward. *Understanding Cultural Differences.* Yarmouth, ME: Intercultural Press, 1990.

Hammond, Phillip, and K. Warner. "Religion and Ethnicity in Late-Twentieth-Century America." *Annals of the American Academy of Political and Social Sciences* 527 (May 1993): 55–67.

Heffer, Jean. "Du 'pull' et du 'push.' " In R. Rougé (ed.), *Les immigrations européennes aux Etats-Unis (1880–1910).* Paris: Presses de l'Université de la Sorbonne (1989), 21–48.

Heffer, Jean, and François Weil (eds.). *Chantiers d'histoire américaine.* Paris: Belin, 1994.

Heller, Monica. "The Role of Language in the Formation of Ethnic Identity." In Jean Phinney and M. J. Rotheram (eds.), *Children's Ethnic Socialization: Pluralism and Development.* Newbury Park, CA: Sage Publications, 1987.

Higonnet, Patrice. "French." In S. Thernstrom et al. (eds.), *Harvard Encyclopedia of American Ethnic Groups*, 379–388. Cambridge: Harvard University Press, 1980.

Hillstrom, Laurie. "French Americans." In *Gale Encyclopedia of Multicultural America*, Vol. I. New York: Gale Research Inc., 1995.

Hoerder, Dirk. "From Migrants to Ethnics: Acculturation in a Societal Framework." In Dirk Hoerder and L. Moch (eds.), *European Migrants: Global and Local Perspectives*. Boston: Northern University Press, 1996.

Kivisto, Peter (ed.). *The Ethnic Enigma*. Philadelphia, PA: The Balch Institute Press, 1989.

Kunz, Virginia. *The French in America*. Minneapolis, MN: Lerner Publications Company, 1966.

Lieberson, Stanley, and Mary Waters. *From Many Strands: Ethnic and Racial Groups in Contemporary America*. New York: Russell Sage, 1988.

Le Menestrel, Sara. *La voie des Cadiens. Tourisme et identité en Louisiane*. Paris: Belin, 1999.

Lindenfeld, Jacqueline. "Bilingualisme et biculturalisme: les Français de la côte ouest des Etats-Unis." *Langage et Société* 73 (1995): 67–83.

———. "Language Contact: A Case Study of French Americans in California and Oregon." In Jane Hill et al. (eds.), *The Life of Language: Papers in Honor of William Bright*, 87–100. Berlin: Mouton de Gruyter, 1997.

———. "Parental Factors in Incipient French-American Bilingualism." *Education et Sociétés Plurilingues* 2 1997: 67–72.

Martin, Philip, and Jonas Widgren. "International Migration: A Global Challenge." *Population Bulletin* 51, no. 1, (1996): 2–38.

Maxwell, Thomas. *The Invisible French: The French in Metropolitan Toronto*. Waterloo, Ontario: Wilfred Laurier University Press, 1977.

Morrice, Polly. *The French Americans*. New York: Chelsea House Publishers, 1988.

Naylor, Larry. *American Culture: Myth and Reality of a Culture of Diversity*. Westport, CT: Bergin and Garvey, 1998.

——— (ed.). *Problems and Issues of Diversity in the United States*. Westport, CT: Bergin and Garvey, 1999.

Nettelbeck, Colin. *Forever French: Exile in the United States 1939–1945*. New York: St. Martin's Press, 1991.

Park, Robert. *Race and Culture*. New York: Free Press, 1950.

Parker, James. *Ethnic Identity: The Case of the French Americans*. New York: University Press of America, 1983.

Pedraza, Silvia, and Rubén Rumbaut (eds.). *Origins and Destinies: Immigration, Race, and Ethnicity in America*. Belmont, CA: Wadsworth, 1996.

Péloquin-Faré, Louise. *L'identité culturelle: Les Francos-Américains de la Nouvelle-Angleterre*. Paris: Didier, 1983.

Petersen, William. *Concepts of Ethnicity*. Cambridge: Harvard University Press, 1980.

Platt, Polly. *French or Foe? Getting the Most Out of Visiting, Living and Working in France*. Skokie, IL: Culture Crossings Ltd., 1995.

Portes, Alejandro, and Rubén Rumbaut. *Immigrant America: A Portrait*, 2d ed. Berkeley, CA: University of California Press, 1996.

Portes, Alejandro, and R. Schauffler. "Language Acquisition and Loss among Children of Immigrants." In S. Pedraza and R. Rumbaut (eds.), *Origins and Destinies: Immigration, Race, and Ethnicity in America*. Belmont, CA: Wadsworth, 1996.

Prévos, André. "French." In D. Levinson and M. Ember (eds.), *American Immigrant Cultures: Builders of a Nation*. New York: Simon and Schuster Macmillan, 1997.

Ramirez, Bruno, and François Weil. "French, French Canadians and Cajuns." In E. Barkan (ed.), *Our Multicultural Heritage*. Westport, CT: Greenwood Press, 1998.

Royce, Anya Peterson. *Ethnic Identity: Strategies of Diversity*. Bloomington, IN: Indiana University Press, 1982.

Spindler, George, and Louise Spindler. *The American Cultural Dialogue and Its Transmission*. Bristol, PA: Falmer Press, 1993.

Stebbins, Robert. *The Franco-Calgarians: French Language, Leisure, and Linguistic Lifestyle in an Anglophone City*. Toronto: University of Toronto Press, 1994.

Thernstrom, Stephan, Ann Orlov, and Oscar Handlin (eds.). *Harvard Encyclopedia of American Ethnic Groups*. Cambridge: Harvard University Press, 1980.

Thompson, Richard. *Theories of Ethnicity: A Critical Appraisal*. New York: Greenwood Press, 1989.

U.S. Department of Commerce. *Statistical Abstract of the United States, 1997*. Washington, D.C.: U.S. Government Printing Office, 1997.

Valdman, Albert (ed.). *French and Creole in Louisiana*. New York: Plenum Press, 1997.

Varro, Gabrielle. *The Transplanted Woman: A Study of French-American Marriages in France*. New York: Praeger Publishers, 1988.

———. "Does Bilingualism Survive the Second Generation? Three Generations of French-American Families in France." *International Journal of the Sociology of Language* 133 (1998): 105–128.

Varro, Gabrielle, and Sally Boyd (Issue eds.). Introduction. *Americans in Europe—A Sociolinguistic Perspective: Probes in Northern and Western Europe*. International Journal of the Sociology of Language 133 (1998): 1–30.

Veltman, Calvin. *L'avenir du français aux Etats-Unis*. Montréal: Bibliothèque Nationale du Québec, 1987.

Waddell, Eric. "French Louisiana: An Outpost of *l'Amérique Française* or Another Country and Another Culture?" In Dean Louder and E. Waddell
(eds.), *French America: Mobility, Identity, and Minority Experience
across the Continent*. Baton Rouge, LA: Louisiana University Press,
1993.

Waters, Mary. *Ethnic Options: Choosing Identities in America*. Berkeley, CA:
University of California Press, 1990.

———. "Optional Ethnicities: For Whites Only?" In S. Pedraza and R. Rumbaut (eds.), *Origins and Destinies: Immigration, Race and Ethnicity in
America*. Belmont, CA: Wadsworth, 1996.

Weil, François. *Les Franco-Américains, 1860–1980*. Paris: Belin, 1989.

Yancey, William, Eugene Ericksen, and Richard Juliani. "Emergent Ethnicity:
A Review and Reformulation." *American Sociological Review* 41, no. 3
(1976): 391–402.

Zeitlin, Theodore. *The French*. London: The Harvill Press, 1995.

Index

About the Author

JACQUELINE LINDENFELD is Lecturer of Anthropology, Sonoma State University, California.